More Hot Illustrations for Youth Talks

100 more attention-getting stories, parables and anecdotes

Wayne Rice

Youth Specialties

ZondervanPublishingHouse

Grand Rapids, Michigan

A Division of HarperCollinsPublishers

More Hot Illustrations for Youth Talks:
Copyright © 1995 by Youth Specialties, Inc.

Youth Specialties Books, 1224 Greenfield Drive, El Cajon,
California 92021, are published by Zondervan Publishing House,
5300 Patterson, S.E., Grand Rapids, Michigan 49530.

Library of Congress Cataloging-in-Publication Data

     More hot illustrations for youth talks: 100 more attention-
getting stories, parables, and anecdotes / [compiled by]
Wayne Rice.
        p.   cm.
  "Youth Specialties."
  Includes index.
  ISBN 0-310-20768-1
  1. Youth sermons—Outlines, syllabi, etc. 2. Homiletical
illustrations. I. Rice, Wayne.
BV4310.M67 1995
251.08—dc20   95–35691
                                             CIP
Unless otherwise noted, all Scripture references are taken from
the Holy Bible: New International Version (North American
Edition), copyright 1973, 1978, 1984 by the International Bible
Society. Used by permission of Zondervan Bible Publishers.

Edited by Noel Becchetti and Lorraine Triggs
Typography and Design by J. Steven Hunt
Printed in the United States of America

ISBN: 0-310-20768-1

    99 00 01 02 / ML / 17 16 15 14 13 12 11 10 9 8

More Hot Illustrations for Youth Talks

YOUTH SPECIALTIES TITLES

Professional Resources

Developing Student Leaders
Developing Spiritual Growth in Junior High Students
Equipped to Serve
Help! I'm a Volunteer Youth Worker!
Help! I'm a Sunday School Teacher!
How to Recruit and Train Volunteer Youth Workers
The Ministry of Nurture
One Kid at a Time
Peer Counseling in Youth Groups
Advanced Peer Counseling in Youth Groups

Discussion Starter Resources

Get 'Em Talking
High School TalkSheets
Junior High TalkSheets
High School TalkSheets: Psalms and Proverbs
Junior High TalkSheets: Psalms and Proverbs
More High School TalkSheets
More Junior High TalkSheets
Parent Ministry TalkSheets
Would You Rather . . . ?

Ideas Library

Ideas Combo 1-4, 5-8, 9-12, 13-16, 17-20, 21-24, 25-28,
29-32, 33-36, 37-40, 41-44,
45-48, 49-52, 53, 54, 55
Ideas Index

Youth Ministry Programming

Compassionate Kids
Creative Bible Lessons in John:Encounters with Jesus
Creative Bible Lessons on the Life of Christ
Creative Programming Ideas for Junior High Ministry
Creative Socials and Special Events
Dramatic Pauses
Facing Your Future
Great Fundraising Ideas for Youth Groups
Great Retreats for Youth Groups
Greatest Skits on Earth
Greatest Skits on Earth, Volume 2
Hot Illustrations for Youth Talks
Hot Talks

Junior High Game Nights
More Junior High Game Nights
Play It! Great Games for Groups
Play It Again! More Great Games for Groups
Road Trip
Super Sketches for Youth Ministry
Teaching the Bible Creatively
Up Close and Personal: How to Build Community in Your
    Youth Group

Clip Art

ArtSource Volume 1—Fantastic Activities
ArtSource Volume 2—Borders, Symbols, Holidays, and
    Attention Getters
ArtSource Volume 3—Sports
ArtSource Volume 4—Phrases and Verses
ArtSource Volume 5—Amazing Oddities and
    Appalling Images
ArtSource Volume 6—Spiritual Topics
ArtSource Volume 7—Variety Pack

Video

Edge TV
God Views
The Heart of Youth Ministry: A Morning with
    Mike Yaconelli
Next Time I Fall in Love Video Curriculum
Promo Spots for Junior High Game Nights
Understanding Your Teenager Video Curriculum
Witnesses

Student Books

Going the Distance
Grow for It Journal
Grow for It Journal Through the Scriptures
Next Time I Fall in Love
101 Things to Do During a Dull Sermon

TABLE OF CONTENTS

Introduction

Nathan the prophet was the guest speaker. King David was the audience. Nathan had a message from the Lord to deliver to David, and, being the excellent communicator that he was, he opened with a story:

There were two men in a certain town, one rich and the other poor. The rich man had a very large number of sheep and cattle, but the poor man had nothing except one little ewe lamb he had bought. He raised it, and it grew up with him and his children. It shared his food, drank from his cup, and even slept in his arms. It was like a daughter to him.

Now a traveler came to the rich man, but the rich man refrained from taking one of his own sheep or cattle to prepare a meal for the traveler who had come to him. Instead, he took the ewe lamb that belonged to the poor man and prepared it for the one who had come to him (II Samuel 12:1-4).

The story, of course, had King David on the edge of his seat. He took it seriously and responded with gut-wrenching emotion: "As surely as the Lord lives, the rich scoundrel who took that little lamb deserves to die!" Bingo. The rest of Nathan's message required few words. All he had to do was apply the story to his audience: "You, sir, are that man."

Nathan knew what every good speaker and teacher knows: a picture is worth a thousand words. A captivating illustration that is thoughtfully chosen and skillfully used communicates more, is remembered longer, and has greater impact than thousands of words that may be truthful and important, but which are abstract and tell no story. Jesus know the value of a story, too. He spoke in parables. In fact, Matthew 13:34 recorded that Jesus never spoke without using a parable. He consistently sprinkled his talks with stories and illustrations to drive home the point he was making. He drew his illustrations from everyday life in the Middle East, describing farmers and families, sheep and goats, barns and wheat fields. People were amazed at his teaching.

Unfortunately, amazing is not often the word that teens use to describe speakers and teachers in the church today. The word "boring" seems to be more in fashion. A few popular speakers, however, know how to communicate well with kids, and invariably they use stories and illustrations effectively in their talks.

Hot Illustrations is a selection of stories that have been used effectively in youth talks by several of those popular speakers. I have used many of them myself. All of them can work with kids if the stories are chosen properly and communicated with conviction and purpose.

This is not an exhaustive collection of illustrations for youth talks. The books that claim to be exhaustive are often so large that they are difficult to use. One book on my shelf boasts nearly eight thousand illustrations in it. But to be honest, it's difficult to find one good illustration in that book when I need it. My goal for this book has been to offer you quality rather than quantity.

Selecting and using illustrations is a subjective and personal task; what works for you may not work for me (and vice versa). Even so, this book offers you a sampling of illustrations that I recommend without reservation. Much of that has to do with the quality of people who contributed to this book (their names are listed on pages 186 and 187). Good illustrations are extremely valuable and hard to come by. Many speakers prefer keeping them to themselves. That's why I'm grateful for these contributors who were willing to share some of their best illustrations with us.

How to Choose and Use Illustrations

Aim to Hit Your Target

The most important thing to remember as you use the illustrations in this book is that they are only illustrations. They are not the points to be made. In other words, don't build your talk around these or any other illustrations. Begin with the point (the truth) that you want to communicate, and then find or create the illustration that supports that point.

A young boy received a bow and arrow from his father and immediately went outside to shoot it. A few minutes later, his father went outside and saw that the boy had shot his arrows at several targets that had been drawn on the side of a fence. To his amazement, each arrow had hit a bull's-eye. The father was impressed and said to his son, "I didn't realize you were such a good shot!" The boy replied, "Oh, it was easy. I shot the arrows first; then drew the targets around them."

When you use illustrations simply because they are good illustrations, you are drawing targets around your arrows. Begin planning a talk by deciding what the point (the target) is. Enhance the talk with an illustration only if it effectively drives home that point. Keep in mind that it takes different kinds of arrows to hit different kinds of targets. In the same way, be selective in filling your quiver with illustrations.

With each illustration in this book, I have suggested one or two points that can be supported by the illustration. Every illustration has multiple applications. A list of general topics that will help you select illustrations more easily can be found on page 181.

Don't Over-Illustrate

Some points are so obvious that they don't need to be illustrated at all.

The truth of the above sentence may not be obvious, so I will illustrate. Suppose I stood up in front of a group and said, "God is good." The truth of that statement may not be clear to some people, so I would illustrate it with a story, example, or analogy that makes a picture in the listeners' minds that describes exactly what I mean when I say "God is good." On the other hand, if the temperature in the room is forty degrees, and I say to the group, "This room is cold," then I probably don't need to illustrate the truth of that statement with a story about someone freezing to death. My audience is not stupid; they know what I mean. The statement is self-evident. To illustrate would belabor the point.

Along with using illustrations only when necessary, use illustrations sparingly. One good illustration per point is plenty. People remember one illustration and may think about it for quite some time. You may remember, for instance, the one joke your friend told you over lunch—you may even tell it yourself to a few other friends. If your friend tells you two jokes, however, by the time you're done laughing at the second joke, you will have in all likelihood already forgotten the first one.

Remembering illustrations works the same way. If you use two or more illustrations, one right after another in the same talk, your audience is likely to forget them quickly. I recently listened to a speaker use twenty or more illustrations in one evening. Although he was entertaining, afterward I couldn't remember any of his illustrations. More significantly, I couldn't remember the point of any of them.

Choose your illustrations wisely. Make your point and illustrate it well, then move on to another point—or just stop. Don't pile illustration on illustration for the same point. Illustration-using is like driving a nail with a hammer—once the nail is in all the way, you stop pounding or you'll leave hammer marks in the wood. Some speakers leave hammer marks on their audiences by over-illustrating their points.

Don't Over-apply Your Illustration

Audiences feel insulted when a speaker does all their thinking for them. You may assist your audience to get your point by proclaiming it as clearly as possible—like Nathan the prophet did. On the other hand, had Nathan not applied the illustration when he did, it is likely that David, after thinking about the story for a while, would have figured it out on his own. Nathan's illustration even speaks to us today when we don't limit its application to only King David.

Jesus often told parables and stories without applying them at all. He allowed his audience to think about it for a while and discuss it among themselves. Jesus' own disciples were no doubt stimulated to learn by having to ponder the meaning of the parables. Of course, we are also the beneficiaries of this strategy of the Master Teacher.

Use Illustrations Strategically

The primary reason for using an illustration is to drive home a point, but illustrations can be used for other purposes as well. You may use an illustration strictly for the purpose of holding a group's attention, for example, or for the purpose of providing a change of pace in your talk to make it more interesting.

I'm always amazed to watch how an audience that is dozing off, doodling on pieces of paper, or whispering to each other suddenly becomes alert when the speaker starts telling a story. As if on cue, all heads are raised and every eye is on the speaker. Things quiet down, and the speaker has everyone's undivided attention. Unfortunately, when the story ends, everyone goes back to what he or she was doing. A good speaker avoids this by making his or her application as poignant (without using the word "poignant") and interesting as the story itself. A properly chosen illustration causes the audience to "stay tuned" to discover what the point is.

Illustrations can also be used to set up a point the speaker is about to make. In other words, the illustration may not communicate much truth on its own, but because it's interesting or funny and serves as an icebreaker, it helps the speaker to segue into the point that she or he desires to make. Jokes, of course, are useful for that purpose. For example, I have used *The Zurka Bird* (page 180) to set up a talk on spiritual gifts or just to break the ice for a talk during the Christmas season. Essentially a joke, it shouldn't be taken seriously on its own. Like any other illustration, you need to tie it into your main purpose. The illustration should do some meaningful work.

Although illustrations may be used to hold a group's attention or to get laughs, if those are the only reasons they are used, the audience becomes frustrated and bored. Like the boy who cried "Wolf!" when there was no wolf, audiences eventually tire of speakers who have no content to their messages.

At a recent function I heard a well-known Christian author who is popular on the banquet circuit use dozens of jokes, stories, and illustrations. Although some of the illustrations were entertaining, his talk was disjointed and never went anywhere. He never had a point to make—or if he did, he never developed it so that the audience could remember what it was. He spoke for over an hour, and even though the speaker was extremely funny at times, I could tell that the audience had had enough. They wanted to go home. I concluded that this speaker was basically an insecure person whose primary concern was not to communicate a message, but to make the audience like him. He spent all his time trying to be entertaining rather than helpful. That's okay for a professional comedian, but not for someone who wants to be taken seriously.

Choose the Right Illustration

It goes without saying that you shouldn't use an illustration that is not right for you or your audience. Some of the illustrations in this book need to be communicated with a dramatic flair or with a sense of humor, for instance. If you have a difficult time being dramatic or funny, then you may want to avoid those illustrations. As you consider an illustration, ask yourself, *How comfortable will I feel using this one? Is this me?*

I remember trying to do Bill Cosby impressions when I was younger. I basically made a fool of myself. Why could Bill Cosby be so funny while I was bombing with the same routines? Because I'm not Bill Cosby. I can't be anyone else but me. When I speak to kids, I limit the illustrations I use to those that I feel comfortable with—those I can communicate with credibility and conviction. You may find that some illustrations in this book are difficult for you to communicate in that way. Stay away from them.

On the other hand, there are plenty of good illustrations you can use effectively. Once you select an illustration, rehearse it until you are comfortable with it and can present it convincingly. Memorize it if necessary. There's nothing worse than giving an illustration that makes no sense because you've left out a key element. I know; I've committed that error on more than one occasion. I've launched into an illustration only to discover that I had forgotten the part that made the illustration work. It's hard to go back and salvage the point.

Some of the illustrations in this book are meant to be read to the audience, such as *Melody in F* on page 118. If you wish, photocopy the illustration and take it with you rather than read directly from the book.

Consider Your Audience

Not all illustrations are appropriate for every audience. Although the illustrations in this book were selected because they are, generally speaking, effective with adolescents, that doesn't mean they deal only with adolescent concerns; it means that adolescents understand them and get the point if you communicate the story well.

Most illustrations in this book are stories, because adolescents love stories—particularly those with a lesson to teach. Teens enjoy making the connection between a concrete illustration and an abstract idea. For many youths, making that mental leap is a new and exciting experience, which makes storytelling an excellent way to teach this age group.

Little children love stories too, but they haven't yet developed the intellectual ability to understand metaphoric or symbolic language. It's hard for them to figure out the meaning of an allegory or parable.

If you use an illustration like *Jimmy and the Genie* (page 96) with little children, for example, they will undoubtedly be captivated by it, simply because of the subject matter. But when you make the application—that things we do which seem dull and boring now may actually be extremely valuable to us someday—chances are pretty good they will miss the point entirely. Ask the children what they learned and they'll probably say, "You should always pick up rocks when a Genie tells you to."

Personalize Your Illustrations

Illustrations are sometimes more effective if you personalize them. If you are using the illustration *Alligators in Your Pond* (page 31) for example, you might say, "I've always wanted to visit the Florida Everglades, that is, until I heard someone say that there are wild alligators running around out there. Thanks but no thanks! I'd rather go visit Walt Disney World where all the animals have people inside them . . . intentionally. Alligators are dangerous animals! I heard about a lady in Florida who actually had a pet alligator in her backyard pond . . . " You can personalize a story that way without actually telling a lie.

An inappropriate personalization of a story might start like this: "I know a lady who lives in Florida . . . " —unless, of course, you actually do. Don't lie to make yourself look important, look good, or even look bad. Be honest with your audience and you'll not only be more effective, but you'll have nothing that can come back later to haunt you.

A famous Christian youth speaker recently lost his entire ministry because it was discovered that much of what he had claimed to be true over the years was actually false. Illustrations are not important enough for you to lie for. Limit yourself to telling the truth. Anything short of that is unethical and has no place in the ministry of the church.

On the other hand, most illustrations aren't entirely true to begin with—even those that happened to you. None of the illustrations in this book are absolutely true. Some of them are based on historical events and on the lives of real people in history (such as *The Milkman's Gift* and *Unbaptized Arms*), but they are presented here as illustrations, not history. They have undoubtedly been altered and embellished in order to make them effective illustrations. At best they are only partially true. Tony Campolo likes to wink and say about his illustrations, "Well, if it didn't happen that way, it should have."

Few of the illustrations in this book actually happened. They are simply stories or parables that communicate truth. There's a difference between a true story and a story that communicates truth. It surprises some people that many of the stories Jesus told were not true. They were parables, and parables by definition are fictional. Jesus made those stories up. There never was an actual prodigal son, at least as far as we know. Jesus made up the story to illustrate a point and did it so well that it has become one of the most beloved stories of all time.

While we're dealing with personalizing illustrations, I will address the question of stealing someone else's illustration and using it as if it happened to you, or as if you thought of it. Is that wrong? Is that a form of plagiarism? I believe the answer is yes—sometimes. I know speakers who can hardly use their own talks anymore because people have "stolen" their illustrations and examples and made them their own. Tony Campolo laughs about the time he was about to deliver his famous "It's Friday, but Sunday's Comin'" message to a church and was stopped by the pastor because the pastor said, "My congregation thinks that story happened to me."

The best way to use an illustration associated with someone else is to credit the source. If the above pastor had only said, "Tony Campolo tells a wonderful story about the time he . . . " Of course, that disclaimer might make the illustration less effective than it would have been if it was one's own, in which case it might be a good idea to avoid using it at all. This book contains few personal illustrations from individual speakers unless they are relatively easy to transfer to another speaker. It's difficult to tell someone else's experience in the third person. These are illustrations that anyone can use. Don't worry about crediting the source, unless you feel it's important to do so.

You can also personalize illustrations by adding color to them, changing the details, renaming the characters, and generally making them more interesting to your audience. This is almost always a good idea when you tell a story from the Bible. Kids listen better when they can relate the story with people, places, and events they are familiar with. Teenagers easily identify with the prodigal son if they can imagine him as a high school student who has decided to drop out of school and leave home with his pockets full of cash.

Let the illustrations in this book encourage you to be on the lookout for illustrations that you can draw from your own life experiences and from the life experiences of others. Powerful illustrations can be derived from everyday life or from television, movies, books, magazines, or newspapers. Keep your eyes and ears open, and file away your discoveries for future use.

Your Goal:
Communicate the Truth

Perhaps you have seen the *Far Side* cartoon by Gary Larson that depicts a dog sitting next to her owner with the caption What We Say to Dogs. The owner is reprimanding the dog for her bad behavior with phrases like, "Bad dog, Ginger! I've had it with you! From now on you stay out of the garbage, or I'll take you to the dog pound! Do you understand me, Ginger? Do you?" The next panel shows the same scene with the caption What Dogs Hear. In this version the owner's words are written out to show us what the dog is actually hearing: "Blah blah blah, Ginger! Blah blah blah blah blah, blah blah blah, Ginger, blah blah?"

Sometimes that's what happens when adults speak to kids. We need to keep in mind that our goal is to communicate the truth in such a way that what we say matches up accurately with what our students hear, understand, and apply. We hope that this book will help you to achieve that goal the next time you stand in front of an adolescent audience.

A CANDLE IN THE DARKNESS

Several years ago in Timisoara, Romania, Laszlo Tokes became pastor of Timisoara's small Hungarian Reformed Church. Tokes preached the Gospel boldly, and within two years membership had swelled to five thousand.

But success can be dangerous in a Communist country. Authorities stationed police officers in front of the church on Sundays, cradling machine guns. They hired thugs to attack Pastor Tokes. They confiscated his ration book so he couldn't buy food or fuel. Finally, in December 1989, they decided to send him into exile.

But when police arrived to hustle Pastor Tokes away, they were stopped cold. Around the entrance of the church stood a wall of humanity. Members of other churches—Baptist, Adventist, Pentecostal, Orthodox, Catholic—had joined together to protest.

Though police tried to disperse the crowd, the people held their post all day and into the night. Then, just after midnight, a 19-year-old Baptist student named Daniel Gavra pulled out a packet of candles. He lit one and passed it to his neighbor.

When Tokes peered out the window, he was struck by the warm glow reflecting off hundreds of faces. That moment, he said later, was the "turning point in my life." His religious prejudices evaporated. Here were members of the body of Christ, completely disregarding denominational divisions, joining hands in his defense.

It was a moving testimony to Christian unity.

The crowd stayed all through the night—and the next night. Finally police broke through. They bashed in the church door, bloodied Pastor Tokes' face, then paraded him and his wife through the crowd and out into the night.

But that was not the end.

No, the religious protest led—as it always does—to political protest. The people streamed to the city square and began a full-scale demonstration against the Communist government. Again Daniel passed out his candles.

First they had burned for Christian unity; now they burned for freedom.

This was more than the government could tolerate. They brought in troops and ordered them to open fire on the crowd. Hundreds were shot. Young Daniel felt a searing pain as his leg was blown off. But the people of Timisoara stood bravely against the barrage of bullets.

And by their example they inspired the entire population of Romania. Within days the nation had risen up and the bloody dictator Ceausescu was gone.

For the first time in half a century, Romanians celebrated Christmas in freedom.

Daniel celebrated in the hospital, where he was learning to walk with crutches. His pastor came to offer sympathy, but Daniel wasn't looking for sympathy.

"Pastor, I don't mind so much the loss of a leg," he said. "After all, it was I who lit the first candle."

The candle that lit up an entire country.

✓ APPLICATION

With a candle, a nineteen-year-old boy sparked a revolution that is still being felt today. Romania is a free country thanks to the efforts of people like Daniel Gavra who were willing to put their lives on the line for the sake of the Gospel and for basic human rights.

You can make a difference wherever you are if you are willing to take a stand. Don't wait for everyone else to do it. Be the first to light your candle.

A Case of Mistaken Identity

Little River Community Church was located just down the street from First Memorial Church. Since they were located on the same street in the same town, the two youth groups from the two churches were often competing with each other. They participated in the same softball league, the same basketball league, and had become intense rivals. Little River Community was always trying to outdo First Memorial and vice versa.

One Sunday, following a Bible study on serving others, the youth group at Little River Community Church decided to go out into their community and put their faith into action. The youth pastor organized the kids into "ministry teams" and challenged them go out and to serve others. They could do anything—but they needed to remember: "Do what Jesus would do."

So the youth group from Little River Community Church fanned out into the neighborhood and starting serving. One group washed cars for people up and down the street. Another group pumped gas for free at a self-service gas station. Another group went to a convalescent home and sang songs to the shut-ins who lived there.

After the time was up, all the ministry teams returned to the church and reported what they had done. Each group had stories to tell, as they shared what they learned and how it made them feel.

One of the groups told of how they had gone to serve a woman who lived close to First Memorial Church. When First Memorial, their rival, was mentioned, everyone groaned. "We mowed grass, raked leaves and did yardwork for her," said one of the students. "She was real nice. And after we were through, she invited us in and prayed for us. And then she said, 'You young people from First Memorial Church are always doing such nice things for us old folks.'"

"Oh no!" said the youth pastor. "She thought you were from First Memorial? Well, I hope you set her straight. Did you tell her that you weren't from First Memorial but from Little River Community?"

"Well . . . no we didn't," said the student, surprised by the youth pastor's question. "You told us to do what Jesus would do, didn't you? We decided that Jesus would just keep his mouth shut."

✓ APPLICATION

This true story (the names have been changed) is remarkable because most of us would probably have been quick to let the woman know she was wrong to credit someone else for the work we had done. But the way of Jesus is not concerned with who gets the credit. In fact, the way of Jesus is to actually rejoice in the good fortune of others. It is to put others first, ourselves last.

When we serve, we should not be concerned with getting credit for it, but with glorifying God. He is the one who should receive praise and thanks. The object of service is not to make ourselves look good, but to direct people's attention to God.

A DIET FOR LOSERS

If you are interested in losing weight, I present to you the incredible new "Loser's Diet." Just follow this diet and you are sure to lose.

BREAKFAST
1/2 grapefruit
1 slice whole wheat toast
8 oz. skim milk

LUNCH
4 oz. lean broiled chicken breast
1 cup steamed zucchini
1 Oreo cookie
Herb tea

MID-AFTERNOON SNACK
Rest of the package of Oreos
1 quart rocky-road ice cream
1 jar hot fudge

DINNER
2 loaves garlic bread
Large pepperoni and mushroom pizza
Large pitcher of root beer
2 Snickers bars
Entire frozen cheesecake, eaten directly from freezer

DIET TIPS:

- If no one sees you eat it, it has no calories.

- If you drink a diet soda with a candy bar, they cancel each other out.

- When eating with someone else, calories don't count if you both eat.

- Food used for medical purposes never counts, such as: hot chocolate, toast, and Sara Lee cheesecake.

- If you fatten up everyone else around you, then you look thinner.

- Movie-related foods don't count because they are simply part of the entire entertainment experience and not a part of one's personal fuel.

- Cookie pieces contain no calories. The process of breakage causes calorie leakage.

✓ APPLICATION

This diet sounds a lot like how some people try live the Christian life, doesn't it? We start off great in the morning—maybe even with a little Bible reading and prayer. But then things start to disintegrate and by the end of the day, we discover that we have blown it big time. We rationalize our behavior with statements like "Well, if no one sees me sin, then it's really no big deal." Or, "If I sin with my friends, then it's okay because everyone is doing it."

That kind of Christianity, of course, is just as ridiculous as the "diet for losers." When we commit ourselves to Christ, we commit ourselves to following Jesus over the long haul. As Paul wrote in Philippians 3:14, "I press on toward the goal to win the prize for which God has called me heavenward in Christ Jesus." Paul not only started well, but he ended well. He didn't give up every time the going got a little rough. He didn't try to change the rules. Instead, he hung in there and finished the race. So can you.

A MILLION FROGS

A farmer came into town and asked the owner of a restaurant if he could use a million frog legs.

The restaurant owner was shocked and asked the man where he could get so many frog legs! The farmer replied, "There is a pond near my house that is full of frogs—millions of them. They croak all during the night and are about to drive me crazy!"

So the restaurant owner and the farmer made an agreement that the farmer would deliver frogs to the restaurant five hundred at a time for the next several weeks.

The first week, the farmer returned to the restaurant looking rather sheepish, with two scrawny little frogs. The restaurant owner said, "Well ... where are all the frogs?"

The farmer said, "I was mistaken. There were only these two frogs in the pond. But they sure were making a lot of noise!"

✓ APPLICATION

Next time you hear somebody criticizing or making fun of you, remember it's probably just a couple of noisy frogs.

Also—remember that problems always seem bigger in the dark. Have you ever lain in your bed at night worrying about things which seem almost overwhelming—like a million frogs croaking? Chances are pretty good that when the morning comes, and you take a closer look, you'll wonder what all the fuss was about.

A PICTURE OF GOD

A little boy sat down at the kitchen table with his crayons and a big sheet of blank paper, and he started to draw.

His father, noticing the youngster hard at work at the table, stopped to look. "What are you doing, son?"

"I'm drawing a picture of God," said the little boy.

"But son," said the father, "You can't draw a picture of God. Nobody knows what God looks like."

The little boy thought for a moment and said, "Well—they will when I get through!"

✓ APPLICATION

Most people would agree with the father in the story. No one knows what God looks like. But maybe that's one of the reasons God created us and called us to serve him. He created us "in his own image" so that we could—in a sense—show the world what God looks like. When we are being conformed into the image of his son, Jesus Christ (Romans 8:29), people can see in us a reflection of our Heavenly Father.

All of us have the ability to represent God to the world—and to do it in our own way. You don't need to worry whether your picture of God looks like everybody else's. You are to serve God uniquely, with the gifts and abilities that God has given to you, and when you get through, people will have a little better idea of what God looks like. They will see God in you!

A STRANGER AT THE DOOR

It was a snowy Christmas Eve. Inside the warm house, the Christmas tree was cheerfully ablaze with lights and surrounded by dozens of presents.

The man's wife and children were dressed and ready to leave for church. "Come with us," they urged, for they loved him.

"Not me," he snapped. "I don't believe all that religion garbage."

For many years the man's wife had been trying to tell him about Jesus Christ and the salvation he offers. How God's Son had become a human being in order to show us the way to heaven.

"Nonsense," the man always said.

The family left for church and the man was all alone in his cozy country home. He glanced out the window at the cold snowy scene outside. He turned to warm himself by the fire.

But as he turned, his eyes caught a movement in the snow outside. He looked. Cats! Three young cats walking slowly past his window.

"The fools," he thought. "They'll freeze for sure!" The man put on his hat and coat and opened the door. A blast of wintery air sent a shiver through his body.

"Come here, cats! Come inside where there's warmth and food. You'll die out there." But the cats ran away, frightened by the stranger at the door.

He walked outside. "Come back! Don't be afraid, I want to save you."

But the cats were gone. It was too late.

"Well, I did everything I could for them," the man muttered to himself. "What more could I do? I'd have to become a cat myself in order to reach them and save them. If I became a cat, I could tell them and show them. They would have to believe me then, unless they were fools."

Just as he reached the door, the church bells rang in the distance. The man paused for a second and listened. Then he went in by the fire, got down on his knees, and wept.

✓ APPLICATION

And that is what the Christmas story is all about. The Creator of the universe loved us so much that he came to earth to show us how to be saved. And if we listen to him and follow him, we will not perish, but instead will be given everlasting life (John 3:16; Philippians 2:6-8).

A Vision of Jesus

Author and speaker Brennan Manning tells the story of a woman who visited her priest and told him that when she prays, she sees Jesus in a vision.

"He appears to me as real as you are standing here right now, Father," said the woman. "And he speaks to me. He tells me that he loves me and wants to be with me. Do you think I'm crazy?"

"Not at all," replied the priest. "But to make sure it is really Jesus who is visiting you, I want you to ask him a question when he appears to you again. Ask him to tell you the sins that I confessed to him in confession. Then come back and tell me what he said."

A few days later the women returned.

"Did you have another vision of Jesus?" the priest inquired of her.

"Yes I did Father," she replied.

"And did you ask him to tell you the sins that I confessed to him while I was in confession?"

"Yes I did," the woman answered.

"And what did he tell you?" asked the priest expectantly.

"He said ... 'I forgot.'"

☑ APPLICATION

Jesus graciously forgives and forgets our sins when we confess them to him. Scripture assures us of this: "If we confess our sins, he is faithful and just to forgive us ..." (1 John 1:9); and "I, even I, am he who blots out your transgressions ... and remembers your sins no more," says the Lord (Isaiah 43:25). Once God has forgiven our sins, they are gone forever, separated from us "as far as the east is from the west" (Psalm 103:12; Hebrews 8:12).

A Visit
from Space

One day a space ship landed in the middle of a huge field just outside a small, rural community. The aliens looked friendly enough, so some farmers cautiously approached them, hoping to establish a good relationship with them. The aliens greeted the earthlings warmly and said, "We are on a mission from the planet Zuron of the galaxy Andromeda. We have been assigned to explore your planet and to discover what you have learned. We are here to learn as much as we can about the planet earth. So tell us, has anything significant happened here on earth that you can tell us about?"

The farmers thought for a moment and then one spoke up and said, "Well we have radio and TV! We can send radio and microwave signals all over the planet using satellites." The aliens replied, "Oh, well we have had that for thousands of years. In fact, that technology has become quite obsolete. What else has happened?"

Again, the farmers scratched their heads and one said, "We have developed computers that can process information in seconds that used to take years. And these computers are small enough to be carried in a briefcase!"

"Well, that's old news, too," said the aliens. "Hasn't anything extraordinary happened here?"

The farmers were still thinking when one of the aliens asked, "We have heard a rumor that God visited your planet many years ago. Is this rumor true?"

"Well, there was a man named Jesus Christ. He claimed . . . "

"Yes! That's it! Jesus Christ! Did he really come?" the aliens asked excitedly.

"Yes," said the farmers, "but . . . "

"What an extraordinary thing! What a *wonderful* thing!" exclaimed the aliens. "Tell us, what did you do when God visited your planet? Did you bring gifts and throw them at his feet? Did you run the streets celebrating and singing? Did all the world finally realize how much he loves them? Please, tell us, what did you do?"

The farmers pondered for a moment and then sheepishly said, "Um . . . we killed him."

✓ APPLICATION

What are you doing with Christ? Are you celebrating? Telling the world? Is he alive in your life and are you enthusiastically living for him?

The Bible says that if we don't praise God and bring glory to him, then the rest of creation will (even aliens from other galaxies, if they exist!). God has visited our planet in the form of his only Son, Jesus Christ. Let's serve him and celebrate!

ALL-POINTS BULLETIN

Thousands of cars are stolen every year in California, but in 1981, there was one car theft that made all the local papers and was the lead story on the evening news. The police had issued an all-points bulletin to find the missing car and to make contact with the person who stole it.

Why was this car theft getting so much attention?

The owner of the stolen car had informed the police that on the front seat of the car was a box of crackers laced with a deadly poison. The car owner had planned to use the crackers as rat bait. So the police were desperately trying to find the thief—not to punish him, but to save his life. They were afraid he would eat one of the crackers and die.

✓ APPLICATION

In the same way, our Heavenly Father pursues us—not because he wants to punish us but because he wants to save us. You may be running away from God because—like the car thief—you are a sinner. You have broken God's law. But what you may not realize is that God is trying to *rescue* you, not condemn you. The penalty for your sin has been paid by Jesus Christ on the cross, and God wants to give you your freedom. So stop running and turn yourself in. Your life is at stake!

ALLIGATORS IN YOUR POND

Several years ago, newspapers carried a story about an elderly lady who lived in the Big Cypress Swamp in South Florida. Her home was an old shack located by a small pond. Every day the lady went out to the pond to draw water.

In the pond lived an alligator. Despite the danger, the lady allowed this alligator to live in the pond for years. It seemed tame. She didn't bother the gator and the gator didn't bother her.

However, one day while she was drawing water from the pond, the gator swam under the water and then plunged up, grabbing the old woman's hand with his mighty jaws. She tried pulling her hand out of his mouth, but the gator ripped it off. Bleeding profusely, the terrified and stunned old woman crawled back to her shack and called for help. Paramedics finally arrived and she received medical attention.

The next day, the park ranger found the alligator in the pond and killed it. When they cut the alligator open, they found the old woman's hand.

The park ranger told reporters, "Alligators are most dangerous when they lose their fear of humans. By allowing an alligator to remain in your pond, you unknowingly give it the courage to attack."

The lady still lives in the swamp. But there are no longer any alligators in her pond.

☑ APPLICATION

Scripture clearly teaches us that the wages of sin is death. Yet too many times, we think we can keep sin in our lives and not suffer the consequences. Eventually it will take a bite out of us.

The writer of Hebrews warned that we must get rid of everything that slows us down, especially sin that distracts us. If we don't, it will handicap us and do damage to the cause of Christ.

What are the alligators living in your pond?

THE ANIMAL SCHOOL

A group of animals got together in the forest one day and decided to start a school. There was a rabbit, a bird, a squirrel, a fish, and an eel. They formed a board of education and tried to create a curriculum.

The rabbit insisted that burrowing in the ground be in the curriculum. The fish insisted on swimming. The squirrel insisted that perpendicular tree climbing be included, and the bird wanted flying.

They put all these courses together and wrote a curriculum guide. Then they insisted that all of the animals take all of the subjects.

Although the rabbit was getting an A in burrowing, perpendicular tree climbing was a real problem for him; he kept falling over backwards. Pretty soon he became brain damaged from these falls, and he couldn't burrow well any more. He found that instead of making an A in burrowing, he was making a C. And, of course, he always made an F in perpendicular climbing.

The bird was really beautiful at flying, but when it came to burrowing in the ground, he couldn't do it so well. He kept breaking his beak and wings. Pretty soon he was making a C in flying as well as an F in burrowing. And he had a very bad time with perpendicular tree climbing.

The squirrel was terrific at perpendicular tree climbing, but was so afraid of the water that he failed swimming altogether.

The fish was easily the best in swimming class, but he wouldn't get out of the water to come to any of the other classes.

The valedictorian of the class was a mentally retarded eel who did everything in a halfway fashion. But the teachers were happy because everybody was taking all the subjects in their broad-based educational curriculum.

(From *Everything You've Heard is Wrong* by Tony Campolo, Dallas: Word, 1992, pg. 130)

✔ APPLICATION

Have you ever felt like the animals in that school? Have you ever been in situation where you are supposed to do things that you are not equipped to do?

The Body of Christ, the church, was designed by God to include everyone, but God never intended for everyone to do everything. You don't have to be like your pastor, or like your youth minister, or like anyone else. God gave you specific abilities—called spiritual gifts—which are to be used in the church and in the world by you and you alone. No one else is gifted quite the way you are, and there are many jobs that only you can do (1 Corinthians 12).

The call to follow Christ is the call to discover our unique giftedness and then to use our God-given gifts and abilities to bring glory and honor to him.

The Antique Vase

A family had in their home a genuine antique vase, which had been handed down to them through several generations. It was a real treasure which was kept on the mantel as a special object of enjoyment.

One day the parents returned home to be greeted at the door by their teenage daughter.

"Mom and Dad," said the daughter, "You know that antique vase that you told us has been passed down from generation to generation?"

"Yes," answered the parents.

"Well, Mom and Dad . . . our generation just dropped it."

✓ APPLICATION

You hear a lot these days about what a mess the world is in. And if you listen to all the news commentators, politicians and writers of books, you get the impression that *your generation* is to blame for it all. Everyone likes to point their fingers at today's young people and wag their heads, as if the present generation is to blame for the world's problems.

But your generation didn't drop it. Our world was broken when Adam and Eve took that fateful first bite out of the forbidden fruit in the Garden of Eden. Sin has been passed to us from generation to generation, and as a result, we see the effects of sin on our world—perhaps more vividly today than ever before.

No, your generation didn't drop it, but your generation does have the power to make the world a better place for the next generation. As followers of Jesus Christ, our mandate is to be salt and light in the world—agents of change on behalf of the kingdom of God.

ARE YOU GOD?

Shortly after World War II came to a close, Europe began picking up the pieces. Much of the Old Country had been ravaged by war and was in ruins. Perhaps the saddest sight of all was that of little orphaned children starving in the streets of those war-torn cities.

Early one chilly morning an American soldier was making his way back to the barracks in London. As he turned the corner in his jeep, he spotted a little boy with his nose pressed to the window of a pastry shop. Inside, the cook was kneading dough for a fresh batch of doughnuts. The hungry boy stared in silence, with his nose pressed against the window, drooling and watching the cook's every move. The soldier pulled his jeep to the curb, stopped, and got out.

"Son, would you like some of those?"

The boy was startled. "Oh yeah . . . I would."

The American stepped inside and bought a dozen, put them in a bag and walked back to where the lad was standing in the foggy cold of the London morning. He smiled, held out the bag and said simply, "Here you are."

As he turned to walk away, he felt a tug on his coat. He looked back and heard the child ask quietly, "Mister . . . are you God?"

✓ APPLICATION

When we love people with no strings attached, we are doing something quite godly. We are demonstrating in a very real way what God is like. God loves us with an unconditional, *agape*, love which is gracious and kind and rare.

Many people find it hard to believe in a God they can't see. They want a God "with skin on." That's why God sent his Son, Jesus—and that's also why he established his church. We are God's agents in the world—and when we are serving others, and loving them with a godly love, we are showing people what God is like. We are helping them to understand that God loves them like we do—only even more so.

Someone once said, "You may be the only Jesus a person ever sees." That's true. As Christians, it is an honor to be able to represent Christ to the world. Let's make sure we represent him accurately.

Bad Luck, Good Luck

An ancient Chinese story:

A farmer had one old horse that he used for tilling his fields. One day the horse escaped into the hills and when all the farmer's neighbors heard about it, they sympathized with the old man over his bad luck. "Bad luck? Good luck? Who knows?" said the farmer.

A week later, the horse returned with a herd of wild horses from the hills and this time the neighbors congratulated the farmer on his good luck. "Good luck? Bad luck? Who knows?" said the farmer.

Then, when the farmer's son was attempting to tame one of the wild horses, he fell off its back and broke his leg. Everyone agreed that this was very bad luck. Not the farmer, who replied, "Bad luck? Good luck? Who knows?"

Some weeks later, the army marched into the village and forced every able-bodied young man to go fight in a bloody war. When they saw that the farmer's son had a broken leg, they let him stay. Everyone was very happy at the farmer's good luck.

"Good luck? Bad luck? Who knows?"

☑ APPLICATION

Life is a lot like that. Sometimes it seems like things are going well, and at other times, things seem to be going badly. And we let those things dictate our feelings and our outlook on life. When things are going well, we're happy and we think God is with us. If they are going badly, we get discouraged and think that God must have abandoned us. We end up being tossed around by our circumstances.

But the apostle Paul wrote in Philippians 4 that he had learned to be content, even happy, in all circumstances. He was happy when things were bad (he was in jail at the time), and he was happy when things were going good as well That's the great thing about being part of God's family. We really don't have to worry in our circumstances, because no matter what, we have hope in Christ. "We know that in everything, God works for the good of those who love him" (Romans 8:28).

THE BALLOON MAN

Everywhere he went, the man carried brightly colored balloons. He enjoyed watching them float above his head. And it was easy to hold the string in his hand or wrap it around his wrist and take his colorful balloons wherever he went. The other people where he worked were accustomed to seeing them. They didn't mind; it brightened the office a little. Even at night the balloons would float above the man as he slept.

One day he went to the fair and had a great time. At the fair he could blend into the atmosphere of the rides and lights and noise. Oh, sometimes people tried to buy his balloons, thinking he was a vendor, but of course he wouldn't sell even one.

At one of the booths he filled in a ticket to see if he could win a free ocean cruise. He certainly didn't plan on winning, but it wouldn't hurt to try. Yet two weeks later a telegram came—he had won! He would enjoy great entertainment and the world's finest chef providing his meals. Talk about excited! The man started packing immediately. He was ready to go days before it was time to leave.

On the morning of the big day, he called a taxi and had the driver take him to the dock very slowly. He had to go slowly because the balloons wouldn't all fit in the taxi and he had to hold some of them out the window. At the dock he unloaded his luggage, went aboard ship, and was welcomed by the officials who had planned his trip. They even had someone take his suitcases down to his cabin while he stayed on deck and enjoyed the activity. The ship was crowded. Many people were aboard just to say goodbye to friends. Confetti, horns, streamers—and lots of balloons. He felt right at home.

Eventually the visitors left and the voyage was begun. It was great! Sailing on a big ocean liner was really refreshing. It also made him very hungry. Someone told the balloon man that the evening meal was in just one hour—a welcome relief!

When they rang the bell, he started to walk toward the dining room on the second deck. The aroma of the food was so enticing. There was one problem, though. Whoever had designed the ship hadn't left enough room for a man with a handful of balloons to get down the passageway. You could do it if you released some of the balloons, but the balloon man just couldn't do that. He had seen some crackers and cheese on the upper deck earlier, so he went back and ate that instead. It was good. Maybe not as good as the chef's dinner, but it was good enough. Besides, he had his balloons. That night the sunset was beautiful and it was exciting to walk along the deck. But it sure got cold quickly after that. Sea air not only makes you hungry, it makes you tired as well. He asked one of the ship's crew where his room was, and the crewman took him down a wide hall and opened the door of his cabin.

It was beautiful. They had given him one of the classiest rooms on the ship. He could see that the interior decorating was the best. And the bed looked inviting. Unfortunately, the door to the cabin was so designed that he couldn't get all the balloons in without breaking some. He tried, but it just wouldn't work.

Back on deck he found some blankets and a deck chair. He tied the balloons around his wrist and the arm of the chair and tried to sleep. The next morning he was still tired. All that day he ate crackers and cheese and that night he slept on deck again.

The next morning the balloon man received an engraved invitation from the captain of the ship. He had been invited to sit at the captain's table and enjoy the specialty of the world famous chef. He would prepare it especially for the balloon man. All that day the man watched as the crew made preparations for the evening banquet, and at 8:00 p.m. the ship's bell rang and the passengers began to go to the dining room. The man watched them go. Soon he could hear the murmur of voices, the sound of silverware, and the clink of glasses. The aroma of the food became even more enticing.

He stood at the end of the passageway for some time. Finally he walked to the back of the ship. He could still hear the dinner in progress. He reached in his pocket and felt the engraved invitation. He knew there was a special place reserved for him at the captain's table. Then he looked up at his balloons. It was hard to do, but slowly—very, very slowly (he hadn't unclenched his hand for years)—one at a time he uncurled his fingers. One by one the balloons began to drift away.

As he watched, the wind caught them and blew them out of sight. The man turned and walked down the passageway. That night, as a guest at the captain's table, he enjoyed the finest meal and the best companionship he'd ever known.

✓ APPLICATION

Are you hanging on to a handful of balloons that keep you from being close to Jesus? What are the names of your balloons? Are they friends? Bad habits? Sex? Possessions? Your pride? Your popularity? Maybe it's time to just let those balloons go so that you can enjoy the relationship with Christ that is yours for the taking. "Let us throw off everything that hinders and the sin that so easily entangles us" (Hebrews 12:1).

[Note: It might be effective to allow the youth to blow up and release some balloons that represent the things they are willing to "let go of" so that they can have a closer relationship with Jesus.]

The Beggar's Rags

A beggar lived near the king's palace. One day he saw a proclamation posted outside the palace gate. The king was giving a great dinner. Anyone dressed in royal garments was invited to the party.

The beggar went on his way. He looked at the rags he was wearing and sighed. Surely only kings and their families wore royal robes, he thought.

Slowly an idea crept into his mind. The audacity of it made him tremble. Would he dare?

He made his way back to the palace. He approached the guard at the gate. "Please, sire, I would like to speak to the king."

"Wait here," the guard replied.

In a few minutes he was back. "His majesty will see you," he said, and led the beggar in.

"You wished to see me?" asked the king.

"Yes, your majesty. I want so much to attend the banquet, but I have no royal robes to wear. Please, sir, if I may be so bold, may I have one of your old garments so that I, too, may come to the banquet?"

The beggar shook so hard that he could not see the faint smile that was on the king's face.

"You have been wise in coming to me," the king said. He called to his son, the young prince. "Take this man to your room and array him in some of your clothes."

The prince did as he was told and soon the beggar was standing before a mirror, clothed in garments that he had never dared hope for.

"You are now eligible to attend the king's banquet tomorrow night," said the prince. "But even more important, you will never need any other clothes. These garments will last forever."

The beggar dropped to his knees. "Oh, thank you," he cried. But as he started to leave, he looked back at his pile of dirty rags on the floor. He hesitated. What if the prince was wrong? What if he would need his old clothes again? Quickly he gathered them up.

The banquet was far greater than he had ever imagined, but he could not enjoy himself as he should. He had made a small bundle of his old rags and it kept falling off his lap. The food was passed quickly and the beggar missed some of the greatest delicacies.

Time proved that the prince was right. The clothes lasted forever. Still the poor beggar grew fonder and fonder of his old rags.

As time passed people seemed to forget the royal robes he was wearing. They saw only the little bundle of filthy rags that he clung to wherever he went. They even spoke of him as the old man with the rags.

One day as he lay dying, the king visited him. The beggar saw the sad look on the king's face when he looked at the small bundle of rags by the bed. Suddenly the beggar remembered the prince's words and he realized that his bundle of rags had cost him a lifetime of true royalty. He wept bitterly at his folly.

And the king wept with him.

☑ APPLICATION

We have been invited into a royal family—the family of God. To feast at God's dinner table, all we have to do is shed our old rags and put on the "new clothes" of faith which is provided by God's Son, Jesus Christ.

But we cannot hold onto our old rags. When we put our faith in Christ, we must let go of the sin in our life, and our old ways of living. Those things must be discarded if we are to experience true royalty and abundant life in Christ. "Behold, the old is passed away; the new has come!" (2 Corinthians 5:17).

BLACKOUT!

Still fresh in the memory of many is the huge power failure that involved much of the northeast United States in November, 1965. At 5:18 p.m., New York City went black, as well as much of the entire state. The area affected covered some 80,000 square miles and took in most of seven U.S. states and most of Canada's province of Ontario. Whether it was a generator feeding power at the wrong frequency or a switch thrown in error by some utility company employee was hard to determine.

But the millions of people living in New York and the surrounding area quickly determined that they were without electricity. The lights were out, the power was out, and many were stuck for the night in subway train stations, elevators, and tunnels under the East River.

The blackout left some 200 planes in the air above New York's Kennedy International Airport. They had to be rerouted to airports in other states where runway lights were still burning. Overall loss in business due to the blackout, which lasted in some areas up to 13 hours, was estimated at $100 million dollars. A tire company, for example, lost $50,000 worth of tires when power failed during a critical curing process. A car manufacturer had to throw away 50 engine blocks because high speed drills froze while boring piston holes. Bakeries in New York alone reported a loss of 300,000 loaves of bread, which were spoiled when the power went off.

All in all, modern civilization as Americans and Canadians knew it that November night came to a screeching halt because the power supply on which they were dependent had been cut off.

☑ APPLICATION

The Christian too, has a power supply on which he is completely dependent. As John 16:8-15 points out, the Holy Spirit is our power supply. The Holy Spirit not only does the job of convicting and convincing the world of sin, but also leads us, guides us, and empowers us. But when we cut off the current by quenching the Holy Spirit, his activity ceases and we are living in the flesh. Just as New Yorkers groped around in darkened subways and tunnels under the East River on the night of the biggest blackout they ever experienced, the Christian who dims the power of the Holy Spirit in his life walks about in spiritual weakness. But unlike the victims of the 1965 power failure, we don't need to wait for someone else to turn the power back on. All we have to do is throw the switches marked *faith* and *obedience*, and the spiritual lights will go on again.

THE BRIDGE OPERATOR

There once was a man who worked in a small town as the operator of a drawbridge on a river. A train track ran across the bridge, and the operator's job was to keep the bridge up when no train was coming so that the boats could pass underneath. When a train approached, he was to blow the whistle and let down the bridge.

One sunny Saturday morning, the man brought his seven-year-old son along to work with him. The boy could frolic along the river, skip rocks on the water, chase butterflies, or even try to catch a fish.

Shortly before noon, a passenger train was due to come through the area. The man began to make preparations to let the bridge down so the train could pass safely across the river. As he examined the bridge, he noticed that someone—a small child—had somehow climbed over the guardrail next to the bridge, and was playing at the very spot where the bridge would come down. As he looked closer, he realized with horror that the child was his son. In desperation, he yelled out his son's name, but the sound of the approaching train drowned out his screams. He knew he had to make a quick decision. If he lowered the bridge now his son would die. But if he didn't, all the people on the train would die as the train plunged into the river. He barely had time to think.

As he screamed in agony, the man thrust forward the lever to lower the bridge just as the train arrived. His son died instantly. And as the train passed by, the people just smiled and waved as they passed by the man in the control booth, with his head bowed low, oblivious to what had just taken place.

☑ APPLICATION

Isn't this what God did for us?

46

THE BURNING HUT

The only survivor of a shipwreck washed up on a small, uninhabited island. He prayed feverishly for God to rescue him, and every day he scanned the horizon for help, but none seemed forthcoming. Exhausted, he eventually managed to build a little hut out of driftwood to protect him from the elements, and to store his few possessions.

But then one day, after scavenging for food, he arrived home to find his little hut in flames, the smoke rolling up to the sky. The worst had happened; everything was lost. He was stung with grief and anger. "God, how could you do this to me!" he cried.

Early the next day, however, he was awakened by the sound of a ship that was approaching the island. It had come to rescue him.

"How did you know I was here?" asked the weary man of his rescuers.

"We saw your smoke signal," they replied.

✓ APPLICATION

It is easy to get discouraged when things are going bad. But we shouldn't lose heart, because God is at work in our lives, even in the midst of pain and suffering. Paul wrote, " . . . I have learned the secret of being content in any and every situation, whether well fed or hungry, whether living in plenty or in want" (Philippians 4:12). Paul had confidence that good would come out of everything (Romans 8:28), so he learned to be thankful, not bitter, even when he was suffering. Who knows? Remember next time your little hut is burning to the ground—it just may be a smoke signal that summons the grace of God.

BUT IS HE SAFE?

The following dialogue appears in C.S. Lewis'*The Chronicles of Narnia* (1961, MacMillan, 1950, C.S. Lewis PTE. LTD.). In *The Lion, the Witch and the Wardrobe,* Susan and Lucy ask Mr. and Mrs. Beaver to describe Aslan. They ask if Aslan is a man. Mr. Beaver replies.

"Aslan a man? Certainly not. I tell you he is the King of the wood and the song of the great Emperor-beyond-the-Sea. Don't you know who is the King of Beasts? Aslan is a lion—*the* Lion, the great Lion."

"Ooh!" said Susan. "I'd thought he was a man. Is he–quite safe? I shall feel rather nervous about meeting a lion."

"That you will, dearie, and make no mistake," said Mrs. Beaver, "if there's anyone who can appear before Aslan without their knees knocking, they're either braver than most or else just silly."

"Then he isn't safe?" said Lucy.

"Safe?" said Mr. Beaver. "Don't you hear what Mrs. Beaver tells you? Who said anything about being safe? 'Course he isn't safe. But he's good. He's the King, I tell you."

✓ APPLICATION

In *The Chronicles of Narnia,* Aslan is C.S. Lewis' representation of Jesus Christ. He is depicted as the great lion, the king of wild beasts, who is anything but "safe." But, Lewis adds, he is *good.*

What do you think about Jesus? Have you domesticated him? Is he safe and non-threatening to you and the way you want to live your life? If you have that image of Jesus—the meek and mild Jesus who doesn't make any demands on you, then you have a wrong image of Jesus. He is not safe. But he is good. It takes courage—a radical commitment—to follow Jesus. Christianity is not a religion for sissies. When you give your life to Christ, you put your life on the line. Are you willing?

The Call of the Barnyard

A flock a wild ducks were flying in formation, heading south for the winter. They formed a beautiful V in the sky, and were admired by everyone who saw them from below.

One day, Wally, one of the wild ducks in the formation, spotted something on the ground that caught his eye. It was a barnyard with a flock of tame ducks who lived on the farm. They were waddling around on the ground, quacking merrily and eating corn that was thrown on the ground for them every day. Wally liked what he saw. "It sure would be nice to have some of that corn," he thought to himself. "And all this flying is very tiring. I'd like to just waddle around for awhile."

So after thinking it over a while, Wally left the formation of wild ducks, made a sharp dive to the left, and headed for the barnyard. He landed among the tame ducks, and began to waddle around and quack merrily. He also started eating corn. The formation of wild ducks continued their journey south, but Wally didn't care. "I'll rejoin them when they come back north in few months," he said to himself.

Several months went by and sure enough, Wally looked up and

spotted the flock of wild ducks in formation, heading north. They looked beautiful up there. And Wally was tired of the barnyard. It was muddy and everywhere he waddled, nothing but duck doo. "It's time to leave," said Wally.

So Wally flapped his wings furiously and tried to get airborne. But he had gained some weight from all his corn-eating, and he hadn't exercised his wings much either. He finally got off the ground, but he was flying too low and slammed into the side of the barn. He fell to the ground with a thud and said to himself, "Oh well. I'll just wait until they fly south in a few months. Then I'll rejoin them and become a wild duck again."

But when the flock flew overhead once more, Wally again tried to lift himself out of the barnyard. He simply didn't have the strength. Every winter and every spring, he saw his wild duck friends flying overhead, and they would call out to him. But his attempts to leave were all in vain.

Eventually Wally no longer paid any attention to the wild ducks flying overhead. He hardly even noticed them. He had, after all, become a barnyard duck.

✓ APPLICATION

Sometimes we get tired of being wild ducks—followers of Jesus Christ. It's not always easy to be obedient to God and to discipline ourselves to hang in there for the long haul. When we are feeling that way, that's when Satan tempts us to "fall out of formation" and to join the barnyard ducks—the world.

But look what happened to Wally. He thought he would just "check it out" for awhile and then leave when he wanted to. But he couldn't do it. Sin is like that. Sin is a trap, and it has a way of changing us into people we don't even want to become. Eventually we lose touch with who we really are—the sons and daughters of the Most High. We become barnyard ducks.

Chippie's Bad Day

Max Lucado tells the story of a woman who had a parakeet named Chippie. She loved Chippie because he was such a happy little song bird. Chippie's constant chirping just seemed to brighten her day.

One day, the woman was cleaning the bottom of Chippie's cage with a vacuum cleaner when the telephone rang. She reached for the telephone without removing the nozzle of the vacuum cleaner from the cage, which was a mistake. The vacuum cleaner nozzle got pointed in the direction of poor little Chippie, and he was suddenly sucked up into the machine.

When the woman looked back at the cage and realized what had happened, she was horrified. She dropped the telephone, turned off the vacuum cleaner and ripped open the dust bag to get to her little bird. Chippie was a real mess, but he was still alive. She raced to the kitchen sink and turned the water on full force on Chippie. The more she tried to wash him, the worse he looked, so she took him to the bathroom and started trying to dry Chippie with her hair dryer—full force and high heat. Finally, she got the bird dry and put him back in his cage.

Several days later, a friend called and asked how Chippie was doing.

"He's alive," she said, "but he just sits in his cage and stares out into space. And," she added thoughtfully, "Chippie doesn't sing much anymore."

✓ APPLICATION

We all know people who are a lot like Chippie. We know young people who once had a song in their hearts. But due to circumstances out of their control, they discovered that "life sucks." As a result, they aren't singing much anymore.

Have you ever felt a little like Chippie? Have you been abused by people you loved? Has your world been turned upside down? Have you lost your desire to sing?

As Chippie found out, there are no "quick fixes." Healing takes time. But there is someone who can give you back your song and restore your joy. His name is Jesus. "Sing to the Lord a new song, for he has done marvelous things" (Psalm 98:1).

THE DEAD CAT

A couple were on their way to a luncheon at a restaurant in an area mall. As they were driving on a curvy road, they ran over a cat. They stopped the car in this residential section and were tempted to just drive on. However, they felt they needed to tell someone, so they went up to the home near where the cat was laying and told the resident of the home what had happened. It was the owner of the cat. The people who ran over the cat asked if there was anything they could do. The elderly resident asked if they would take care of disposing of the body of the cat. They went back out to the street and picked the dead cat up and put it in the only bag they had in their car, which was a

Nordstrom's bag (an expensive clothing store). They then decided to keep their luncheon and take the cat to the animal shelter after lunch.

When they arrived at the mall, they parked in front of the restaurant. They took the Nordstrom's bag with the cat in it and laid it on the hood of their car in case it should start to smell. In the restaurant they could see their car. They noticed a Mercedes Benz pull up next to their car and a finely dressed woman get out. The woman saw the Nordstrom's bag, looked around, grabbed the bag without looking in it, and proceeded to walk into the same restaurant the couple were in. This wealthy woman had evidently thought that she had stolen something of great value and placed the bag by her feet after sitting at a table close by the couple. The couple didn't say a word but just watched this lady. The lady ordered her meal and was served. Her curiosity got the better of her and she could not resist looking into the bag to see what expensive item she would find.

She leaned over to peek in the sack and fainted dead away.

The manager called an ambulance which arrived within minutes from its station a couple of blocks away. The ambulance attendants gathered up the woman and her personal effects. As they placed the unconscious body into the ambulance, she began to come around just as they placed the Nordstrom's bag containing the dead cat onto the middle of her chest.

☑ APPLICATION

". . . You can be sure that your sin will find you out" (Numbers 32:23).

DESERT PETE

Many years ago, a weary traveler hiked for miles across the desert with the hot sun beating down on his back. His water supply was gone, and he knew that if he didn't find water soon to quench his thirst, he would surely die.

In the distance, he spotted a deserted cabin which brought hope that maybe water was to be found there. He made his way to the cabin and discovered an old well. He frantically pumped the handle of the well to draw water, but all that came from the pump was dust.

Then he noticed a tin can tied to the pump, with a note inside. The note said:

Dear stranger:

This pump is all right as of June 1932. I put a new sucker washer in it, and it should last for quite a few years. But the washer dries out and the pump needs to be primed. Under the white rock, I buried a jar of water, out of the sun and corked up. There's enough water in it to prime the pump, but not if you drink some first. Pour about 1/4 of the water into the pump and let her soak for a minute to wet the leather washer. Then pour the rest medium fast and pump hard. You'll get water. Have faith. This well has never run dry.

When you get watered up, fill the bottle and put it back as you found it for the next stranger who comes this way.

Pete

✓ APPLICATION

Would you have faith to pour the jar of water into the well as the note instructed?

Jesus said, "Whoever finds his life will lose it, and whoever loses his life for my sake will find it" (Matthew 10:39). The same principle applies here. If you live your life selfishly, you will surely die. But if you give yourself away ("lose your life" for the sake of the Gospel) you will live. Your thirst for happiness and fulfillment will be met.

In his note, Desert Pete wrote, "This well has never run dry." Likewise, God is faithful and his promises are true. He has never failed those who have trusted him.

THE DEVIL'S TRIANGLE

At 2:10 p.m. on December 5, 1945, five U.S. Navy planes took off in clear weather from Fort Lauderdale, Florida and flew east over coastal waters. Squadron 19 included Lt. C.C. Taylor commanding four student pilots along with their crews—fourteen men, all of them involved on a navigational training mission between Florida and the Bahamas.

At 3:40 p.m., Taylor reported that his gyro and magnetic compass were not responding properly. Squadron 19 followed the leader aimlessly, first east, then west, then northeast, over the ocean, as Lieutenant Taylor tried to get his bearings by radio.

Then, suddenly, Flight Commander Taylor gave quick orders to ditch, to bail out. And, not long after that, all contact was lost.

Quickly, two Martin Mariner sea planes—giant aircraft designed for long range patrols—were dispatched to search for Squadron 19. After several hours, the wind kicked up to thirty knots, visibility became limited, and a return to base was ordered. Only one of the Mariner sea planes landed.

For days following, the Navy and Coast Guard combed a 100,000-square-mile area with more than one hundred planes and surface craft. But even to this day, there has never been found a trace of the five aircraft in Squadron 19 or the giant Mariner sea plane.

In the same mysterious way, two years later, on January 30, 1947, a British commercial airliner called the Star Tier, with thirty-one passengers aboard, vanished after radioing Bermuda that all was well and that landing would be precisely on schedule.

More recently, on December 22, 1967, the twenty-three-foot cabin cruiser *Witchcraft* disappeared off the coast of Miami after reporting propeller problems. Ten minutes after receiving the report, the Coast Guard arrived on the scene—but no sign of the cruiser has ever been found.

Similar episodes are found in government files regarding some forty ships and twenty planes which have mysteriously disappeared over the last century in a southwestern quadrant of the North Atlantic often referred to as the Bermuda Triangle or the Devil's Triangle.

There have been a number of plausible explanations over the years to explain just what does occur in this geographical triangle that touches Bermuda, Puerto Rico and a point in the Gulf of Mexico west of Florida—everything from the scientific to the mystical—and still no one really knows what happened.

☑ APPLICATION

It is doubtful that any of us will fall victim to the Devil's Triangle.

At least not *that* one . . .

But there is another, more dangerous Devil's Triangle that remains a threat to every single one of us. It is a Devil's Triangle that causes more Christians to bail out and to mysteriously disappear than any part of the world's geography. And, unfortunately, this triangle is no myth, no fable—and there is no way to explain it away.

It is a Devil's Triangle about which the Scripture warns us with grave care and concern. Simply stated in 1 John 2:15-17, this triangle includes three key coordinates: "the lust of the eyes, the lust of the flesh, and the pride of life."

The lust of the eyes is the desire to have all that the world offers. The lust of the flesh is the desire to do what the world does. And the pride of life is the desire for the world's approval rather than the approval of God. Scripture warns us: "If anyone loves the world, the love of God is not in him . . . The world and its desires pass away, but he who does the will of the Father lives forever." Don't be caught in the Devil's Triangle.

The Emperor's Seeds

Once there was an emperor in the Far East who was growing old and knew it was coming time to choose his successor. Instead of choosing one of his assistants or one of his own children, he decided to do something different. He called all the young people in the kingdom together one day. He said, "It has come time for me to step down and to choose the next emperor. I have decided to choose one of you." The kids were shocked! But the emperor continued. "I am going to give each one of you a seed today. One seed. It is a very special seed. I want you to go home, plant the seed, water it, and come back here one year from today with what you have grown from this one seed. I will then judge the plants that you bring to me, and the one I choose will be the next emperor of the kingdom!"

There was one boy named Ling who was there that day and he, like the others, received a seed. He went home and excitedly told his mother the whole story. She helped him get a pot and some planting soil, and he planted the seed and watered it carefully. Every day he would water it and watch to see if it had grown. After about three weeks, some of the other youths began to talk about their seeds and the plants that were beginning to grow.

Ling kept going home and checking his seed, but nothing ever grew. Three weeks, four weeks, five weeks went by. Still nothing. By now all the others were talking about their plants but Ling didn't have a plant, and he felt like a failure. Six months went by—still nothing in Ling's pot. He just knew he had killed his seed. Everyone else had trees and tall plants, but he had nothing. Ling didn't say anything to his friends, however. He just kept waiting for his seed to grow.

A year finally went by and all the youths of the kingdom brought their plants to the emperor for inspection. Ling told his mother that he wasn't going to take an empty pot. But she encouraged him to go, and to take his pot, and to be honest about what happened. Ling felt sick to his stomach, but he knew his mother was right. He took his empty pot to the palace.

When Ling arrived, he was amazed at the variety of plants grown by all the other youths. They were beautiful—in all shapes and sizes. Ling put his empty pot on the floor and many of the other kids laughed at him. A few felt sorry for him and just said, "Hey, nice try."

When the emperor arrived, he surveyed the room and greeted the young people. Ling just tried to hide in the back. "My, what great plants, trees, and flowers you have grown," said the emperor. "Today, one of you will be appointed the next emperor!"

All of a sudden, the emperor spotted Ling at the back of the room with his empty pot. He ordered his guards to bring him to the front. Ling was terrified. "The emperor knows I'm a failure! Maybe he will have me killed!"

When Ling got to the front, the Emperor asked his name. "My name is Ling," he replied. All the kids were laughing and making fun of him. The emperor asked everyone to quiet down. He looked at Ling, and then announced to the crowd, "Behold your new emperor! His name is Ling!"

Ling couldn't believe it. Ling couldn't even grow his seed. How could he be the new emperor?

Then the emperor said, "One year ago today, I gave everyone here a seed. I told you to take the seed, plant it, water it, and bring it back to me today. But I gave you all boiled seeds which would not grow. All of you, except Ling, have brought me trees and plants and flowers. When you found that the seed would not grow, you substituted another seed for the one I gave you. Ling was the only one with the courage and honesty to bring me a pot with my seed in it. Therefore, he is the one who will be the new emperor!"

✓ APPLICATION

"I tell you the truth, unless a kernel of wheat falls to the ground and dies, it remains only a single seed. But if it dies, it produces many seeds. The man who loves his life will lose it, while the man who hates his life in this world will keep it for eternal life" (John 12:24-5). This scripture reminds us that the person who is willing to take less now will receive more later. By "dying" to ourselves now, we live forever.

Jesus said, "Not everyone who says to me, 'Lord, Lord,' will enter the kingdom of heaven, but only he who does the will of my Father who is in heaven" (Matthew 7:21). It's not enough to just look like a Christian on the outside. Jesus wants us to be genuine.

The Empty Chair

Brennan Manning tells the following story of an old man was dying of cancer.

The man's daughter had asked the local priest to come and pray with her father. When the priest arrived, he found the man lying in bed with his head propped up on two pillows and an empty chair beside his bed. The priest assumed that the old fellow had been informed of his visit. "I guess you were expecting me," he said.

"No, who are you?"

"I'm the new associate at your parish," the priest replied. "When I saw the empty chair, I figured you knew I was going to show up."

"Oh yeah, the chair," said the bedridden man. "Would you mind closing the door?"

Puzzled, the priest shut the door.

"I've never told anyone this, not even my daughter," said the man. "But all of my life I have never known how to pray. At the Sunday Mass I used to hear the pastor talk about prayer, but it always went right over my head . . .

"I abandoned any attempt at prayer," the old man continued, "until one day about four years ago my best friend said to me, 'Joe, prayer is just a simple matter of having a conversation with Jesus. Here's what I suggest. Sit down on a chair, place an empty chair in front of you, and in faith see Jesus on the chair. It's not spooky because he promised, 'I'll be with you always.' Then just speak to him and listen in the same way you're doing with me right now.'

"So, Father, I tried it and I've liked it so much that I do it a couple of hours every day. I'm careful, though. If my daughter saw me talking to an empty chair, she'd either have a nervous breakdown or send me off to the funny farm."

The priest was deeply moved by the story and encouraged the old guy to continue on the journey. Then he prayed with him, anointed him with oil, and returned to the rectory.

Two nights later the daughter called to tell the priest that her daddy had died that afternoon.

"Did he seem to die in peace?" he asked.

"Yes, when I left the house around two o'clock, he called me over to his bedside, told me one of his corny jokes, and kissed me on the cheek. When I got back from the store an hour later, I found him dead. But there was something strange, Father. In fact, beyond strange—kinda weird. Apparently, just before Daddy died, he leaned over and rested his head on a chair beside the bed."

(From *Abba's Child* by Brennan Manning, Colorado Springs: NavPress, 1994, pg. 126-7)

✓ APPLICATION

John, who was known as the beloved disciple, wrote twice in his Gospel of the time that he laid his head on Jesus' breast in a moment of intimacy (John 13:23, 25; 21:20). It was a special memory for John, one that assured him that he was indeed a "disciple whom Jesus loved."

Brennan Manning writes, "The Christ of faith is no less accessible to us in his present risenness than was the Christ of history in his human flesh to the beloved disciple." We can have the same kind of relationship with Jesus that John did.

Do you have that kind of relationship with Jesus? Are you and Jesus so close that you can converse with him as you would with a friend? Do you know that he loves you passionately and that he is interested in you and wants to listen to everything that you have to say? Can you lay your head on his breast and feel his heartbeat?

That's the kind of relationship that Jesus wants to have with you.

The Evangelist and the Post Office

A famous evangelist was in town to hold an evangelistic crusade. On the way to the stadium where the crusade was being held, the evangelist wanted to stop at the post office and mail a letter. But he got hopelessly lost and finally decided to ask someone for directions.

He noticed a little boy walking on the sidewalk, so he pulled over and said, "Excuse me, son, but can you tell me where the post office is?"

The little boy said, "Sure. Turn around and go back down the street to the first light, turn left and it's a block or two on your right."

"Thank you very much, young man," said the evangelist. "By the way," he added, handing the boy an announcement for the crusade, "I'd like to invite you to come to a meeting later today where I'll tell you how you can find Jesus Christ as your personal Savior."

"Fat chance," said the little boy. "You can't even find the post office."

✓ APPLICATION

Fortunately for us, we don't have to find Jesus. Jesus finds us. In Luke 15, Jesus describes us as "lost sheep." As a shepherd with a flock of one hundred sheep, he says, he leaves the ninety-nine in order to go out and find the one that has gone astray. We don't have to find our way back to the fold. Jesus is pursuing us. All we need to do is stop running and let him take us back.

"EXCUSE ME" OR "FORGIVE ME"?

If you think drivers come up with some unbelievable excuses when they're trying to talk a cop out of giving them a ticket, you should see the stories that turn up on insurance companies' accident forms. Some time ago *The Toronto Sun* newspaper printed a few samples from actual reports:

"A pedestrian hit me and went under my car."

"In my attempt to kill a fly, I drove into a telephone pole."

"I had been driving my car for forty years when I fell asleep at the wheel and had an accident."

"I had been shopping all day for plants and was on my way home. As I reached an intersection, a hedge sprang up, obscuring my vision. I did not see the other car."

"The pedestrian had no idea which direction to go, so I ran over him."

"The telephone pole was approaching fast. I was attempting to swerve out of its path when it struck my front end."

"Coming home, I drove into the wrong house and collided with a tree I don't have."

"The guy was all over the road. I had to swerve a number of times before I hit him."

"My car was legally parked as it backed into the other vehicle."

"An invisible car came out of nowhere, struck my vehicle, and vanished."

"The indirect cause of this accident was a little guy in a small car with a big mouth."

✓ APPLICATION

Most of us mess up in life and we also have some pretty lame excuses. But the Bible tells us in 1 John 1:9, "If we confess our sins, [God] is faithful and just and will forgive us our sins and purify us from unrighteousness . . . " That's an incredible promise.

But it comes with a premise: "If we confess our sins . . . " Confession comes from a word that means "to call it the same thing." In other words, when we sin, we don't need to make excuses, or blame somebody else, or try to wiggle out of it. We need to say, "God, this was sin. You call it sin; I call it sin, and that's all there is to it. Please forgive me."

It's been said that the only sin God can't forgive is the sin that is never confessed. Every time we take a wrong turn, or find ourselves swerving off the road, we have a choice to make. Will we confess our sin, or ask God to excuse our sin? It boils down to one of two prayers: "God, will you excuse me?" or "God, will you forgive me?"

THE FACE ON THE PUZZLE

A father had just settled into his recliner on Sunday afternoon, looking forward to wading through his six-inch thick newspaper, when his five-year-old son Bobby came scampering into the room. "Daddy! Daddy!" said the boy, "Can you play with me?"

The father tried to be gentle in his response when he told his son, "Bobby, Daddy wants to read his paper for a little while. But if you come back in twenty minutes, we can play together."

Though mildly annoyed at being put off, Bobby rumbled out of the room, leaving his father alone to read his paper.

But five-year-olds have a poor sense of time, so it was only a few short minutes when Bobby was back. "Daddy, can we play now?"

"Not now, Bobby," said the father. "Don't bother me until I'm finished with my paper."

Bobby stomped his way out of the room to wait, but before his father could even get to the sports pages, Bobby returned. He shoved his head up under the paper and said, "Please Daddy, can we play now?"

The father, now convinced that he would never get a moment's peace without giving in, looked on the floor and noticed that there was a full page map of the world included in his newspaper. He reached for his wife's sewing scissors and proceeded to cut the map into about twenty pieces. Leading his son to the kitchen table, he told Bobby to put together this puzzle of the world as the first of their afternoon games. "When you finish the puzzle, then I'll play with you," the father promised. He knew it would take his son a long time to put the puzzle together, and that would give him plenty of time to read his paper.

Not five minutes had passed when Bobby burst back into the room. "Daddy, I'm through with the puzzle! What can we play next?"

"What? You finished already?" asked the father. He got up from his chair and went into the kitchen to look. Sure enough, the puzzle was complete, with every piece in its proper place. "Bobby . . . how did you ever do this so fast? Where did you learn how to do this?" asked the father in amazement.

"It was easy, Daddy." said Bobby. "You see, on the back of the map of the world was a picture of a person. I decided to put the person together first. When I did that, the whole world seemed to fit right into place."

☑ APPLICATION

We live in a broken world in desperate need of being put back together. But it can't be done with social programs, more laws, better schools, the right politicians, or systems of government. The only way to put a broken world together is by putting broken people back together. Changed lives will result in a changed world.

The best thing you can do to impact your world is to lead someone to Jesus Christ. Jesus is the only one who can put broken people back together again. And when a person has been put back together, the whole world seems to fit right into place.

FAKE CHRISTIANS

There was a recent newspaper story about twenty-eight-year-old Mark Carver, a young man who, at the time, was employed as a doctor and as an assistant medical director in a major hospital.

The problem, it seems, was that Mark had never gone to college or medical school. He allegedly forged documents to get the job as a doctor, and knew enough medical gibberish to fool everyone into thinking he was the real thing.

If convicted, he'll spend seven years in jail acting like a prisoner (a position for which he is better qualified).

☑ APPLICATION

Unfortunately, Mark reminds us of a lot of people who call themselves Christians. They go to church. They don't swear or drink a lot. They pray once in a while. They know just enough "Christianese" to pass as the real thing.

But they're just going through the motions. They've never made a personal commitment to Christ.

Paul says that, in the last days, "people will be lovers of themselves, lovers of money, boastful, proud, abusive, disobedient to their parents, ungrateful, unholy, without love, unforgiving, slanderous, without self-control, brutal, not lovers of the good, treacherous, rash, conceited, lovers of pleasure rather than lovers of God" (2 Timothy 3:1-5). Whew! What a list!

He also says that many people will have a form of religion while denying God's power. In other words, they look like Christians on the outside, but they don't have the power on the inside.

Most of us don't want a phony doctor removing our appendix. And God doesn't need any phony Christians. It's not that it's so hard to go through the motions once at week at church, or say the right stuff at youth group. Most of us can probably pull it off for a while.

But why not accept Christ and know the power of genuinely living with him?

FISHING EAGLES

National Geographic aired a special one night about how eagles catch fish in lakes. They fly high above the water but their eyesight is so good they can spot fish in the water below. When they see one they fold back their wings and aim directly for the water, going as fast as 130 mph. When they reach the water they spread their wings, reach out their talons, grab the fish, and begin flying back to the shore.

On this TV special, they showed film of a very unusual occurance. An eagle made a dive for a fish and grabbed it in its talons. But the fish was much larger than the eagle realized. As it began to fly to the shore you could see the strain on the eagle's face. It was not going to make it to the shore with this huge fish. It then tried to drop the fish, to let go of it. But the talons of the eagle had dug into the flesh of the fish so deeply that it could not pull them out. It struggled but to no avail.

Slowly the eagle descended into the lake and drowned, unable to let loose of its catch.

☑ APPLICATION

Many times in life we grab on to something that can be dangerous. We feel we have control and can stop holding on any time we like. It becomes a habit and one day we try to get out and discover that we no longer have a hold of it but it has a hold of us. "Therefore, since we are surrounded by such a great cloud of witnesses, let us throw off everything that hinders and the sin that so easily entangles, and let us run with perseverance the race marked out for us" (Hebrews 12:1).

G.I. LIFE INSURANCE

There was a second lieutenant during World War II who graduated from Harvard University and went into the military. Having been in the R.O.T.C. program, he was very proud of his alma mater and proud of his new position as a second lieutenant. His first assignment was to take a group of raw recruits from the hills of Oklahoma and convince them that they should buy G.I. Life Insurance, a policy that was offered by the U.S. Government that would pay their families $10,000 if they died while on duty. He marched in with his freshly pressed uniform and shining brass, wanting to do well in his first assignment as a second lieutenant in the U.S. Army.

With great eloquence and rhetorical ability he appealed to these men's responsibility, their love of family, and loyalty to country. He came to the end of his presentation and asked for a response. "How many of you will buy G.I. Life Insurance before you go overseas?" Nobody responded.

Well, he was facing failure, but he was a plucky young lad and not one to give up easily. So he redoubled his efforts and with even greater brilliance rose to the occasion and gave a straightforward, clear, convincing presentation as to why they should buy G.I. Life Insurance before they went overseas. And again he came to the close and got no response.

At this point, he lost it and began to share a portion of his mind he could ill afford to lose. The situation was deteriorating rapidly when a wise old master sergeant walked up, put his arm around the second lieutenant's shoulder and said, "Sir, let me speak to the men. I don't think you convinced them they have a need." He turned to the men and said, "Gentlemen, it's like this. You go overseas and you don't buy G.I. Life Insurance and you get a bullet in the head, the government doesn't have to come up with anything. On the other hand, you go overseas and you buy G.I. Life Insurance and you get a

bullet in the head, the government has to come up with ten thousand big ones. Let's go over this again. You go overseas, you don't buy G.I. Insurance, you get a bullet in the head, the government doesn't have to come up with anything. On the other hand, you go overseas, you have G.I. Insurance, you get a bullet in the head, the government has to come up with ten thousand big ones. Now tell me, gentlemen, whom do you think the government will send to the front lines first?"

Well, he sold some life insurance.

✓ APPLICATION

You may be rejecting Jesus Christ because you don't think you need him. You think you can get along fine without him. But you have needs that you don't even realize you have. The French philosopher Blaise Pascal once put it this way: In every human being there is a God-shaped vacuum which only God can fill." You can try to fill that empty place in your life with friends, possessions, sex, popularity, money, achievements—and the void in your life will remain, because only Jesus can satisfy the lonely place in your heart.

Alternate application: As this story demonstrates, you can't sell anything to anyone unless you can show them that they need it. In the same way, you won't be successful sharing Christ with your friends unless you are able to understand their needs and help them to see that Jesus can meet that need.

GET OFF MY BACK

An ancient story is told about a father and his son who were walking along a road one day with their donkey. Soon they met a man who told them how foolish they were to walk when they had a donkey that could be ridden. So the father and son hopped on.

They hadn't gone very far when another man criticized them for both riding on the donkey. They were too heavy for it, he contended, and were being inhumane. So the boy got off.

It wasn't long before a third traveler accused the father of being inconsiderate because he made his son walk while he rode. So the two switched places.

Soon they met another person who charged that the son was not being thoughtful of his father, who was so much older than he.

When last seen, the two were trudging down the road carrying the donkey.

✓ APPLICATION

There is an old rock song that says, "You can't please everyone, so you gotta please yourself." Whom do you try to please? If you listen to the crowd and try to dance to their tune, you will always be frustrated. If you are overly sensitive to the opinions and criticisms of others, you will end up carrying a needless burden of guilt and inadequacy. And if you just try to please yourself, you will become egocentric and selfish.

That's why as Christians, we seek to please God, not other people. Paul wrote, "For me, to live is Christ!" Ultimately, our accountability is to God. "We are not trying to please men but God, who tests our hearts" (1 Thessalonians 2:4).

GOOD GRIEF!

. . . is an example of an oxymoron, a "two-word phrase containing contradictory elements." Here are some more.

"Jumbo shrimp"　　　　　　　　"Negative growth"

"Military intelligence"　　　　　"Postal service"

A "numb feeling"　　　　　　　"Congressional leadership"

"Plastic glasses"　　　　　　　*For golfers:* "Metal Woods"

"Fresh frozen"　　　　　　　　A "little lot"

An "exact estimate"　　　　　　An "unbiased opinion"

A "working vacation"　　　　　"Oddly appropriate"

　　　　　　　　　　　　　　　"Clearly misunderstood"

✓ APPLICATION

There are also religious oxymorons. One of the most common is the term "Lukewarm Christian." These are two words that just don't go together. Scripture says, " . . . because you are lukewarm—neither hot nor cold—I am about to spit you out of my mouth" (Revelation 3:16). Also, "No one can serve two masters. Either he will hate the one and love the other, or he will be devoted to the one and despise the other . . . " (Matthew 6:24).

This doesn't mean that we are perfect Christians (in fact, "Perfect Christian" is an oxymoron in itself). It just means that when we come to Christ, we must be willing to give him our whole selves, not just part of ourselves. When Jesus comes into your life, he can't become "one more thing." Instead, he wants to take over. As the apostle Paul wrote, "Therefore, if anyone is in Christ, he is a new creation; the old has gone, the new has come!" (2 Corinthians 5:17). That's not lukewarm, that's "hot!"

GRAB A WHAT?

There is a college which offers a course called Environmental Science, which is another way of saying it's a class about the outdoors. The class usually includes several field trips, one of which is a long hike in the mountains up several steep trails.

One year, to prepare the students for the hike, the professor gathered all the students in a clearing and asked them to do something very unusual.

"I want you to mingle around and grab each other in the butt," he said. "Just keep grabbing each other in the butt until I tell you to stop."

So about twenty college students started moving among each other, grabbing each others' butts. They were a little nervous about it at first, but after a while it became fun.

After this exercise, the professor told the class the reason for this unusual procedure.

"We are going to be walking up a steep, narrow, slippery slope," he explained. "Because of this, we will have to walk single file, hunched over, using our hands and feet. If the person in front of you should slip, the first thing you'll meet is his or her butt. If that happens, you'll need to reach up with both hands, grab on, and stop him or her from falling. If you aren't used to touching someone's butt, you might be tempted to step aside and let the person slide. This would put him or her at risk, as well as those behind you."

☑ APPLICATION

The same principle applies in the church. We don't grab butts, but we get to know each other well enough that we will be better able to help each other in time of need. That's what the body of Christ is all about. There may be a time when someone has a deep need, and you may be the only person around to give help. If you haven't taken the time to get to know that person, there is a good chance you will just step aside and let the person slide.

GRANDMA'S GIFT

As a ninth grader, Dave was the smallest kid in his high school. But at five feet tall and ninety pounds, he was the perfect candidate for the lightest weight class on the school's wrestling team.

Dave started out as the JV lightweight, but moved up to the varsity position when the boy at that spot moved away.

Unfortunately, Dave's first year was not one for the record books. Of the six varsity matches he wrestled, he was pinned six times.

Dave had a dream of someday being a good enough wrestler to receive his athlete's letter. An athlete's letter is a cloth emblem with the school's initials on it, which is awarded to those athletes who demonstrate exceptional performance in their sports. Those who were fortunate enough to receive a letter proudly wore it on their school letterman jackets.

Whenever Dave shared his dream of "lettering" in wrestling, most of his teammates and friends just laughed. Those who did offer encouragement to Dave usually said something like, "Well, it's not whether you win or lose . . . " or "It's not really important whether you letter or not . . . " Even so, Dave was determined to work hard and keep improving as a wrestler.

Every day after school, Dave was in the weight room trying to build up his strength, or running the stadium bleachers trying to increase his endurance, or in the wrestling room trying to improve his technique.

The one person who continually believed in Dave was his grandmother. Every time she saw him, she reminded him of what could be done through prayer and hard work. She told him to keep focused on his goal. Over and over again, she quoted Scripture verses to him, like "I can do all things through Christ who gives me strength!" (Philippians 4:13).

The day before the next season began, Dave's grandmother passed away. He was heartbroken. If he ever did reach his goal of someday getting a high school letter, his grandmother would never know.

That season Dave's opponents faced a new person. What they expected was an easy victory. What they got instead was a ferocious battle. Dave won nine of his first ten matches that year.

Midway through the season, Dave's coach called him into his office to inform him that he would be receiving his high school letter. Dave was ecstatic. The only thing that could have made him feel better was to be able to share it with his grandmother. If only she knew!

Just then the coach smiled as he presented Dave with an envelope. The envelope had Dave's name written on it in his grandmother's handwriting. He opened it and read:

> Dear Dave,
> I knew you could do it! I set aside $100 to buy you a school jacket to put your letter on. I hope you'll wear it proudly, and remember, "You can do all things through Christ who gives you strength!"
> Congratulations,
> Grandma

After Dave finished reading the letter, his coach reached behind him and pulled out a brand new jacket with the school letter attached and Dave's name embroidered on the front. Dave realized then that his grandmother did know after all.

☑ APPLICATION

Christ does give us the strength to achieve great things, and sometimes the power of Christ comes to us through other people. Dave was motivated to work hard because of the encouragement he received from his grandmother. His grandmother was, in a very real sense, the power of Christ working in his life. Likewise, when we encourage and support one another, we are allowing Christ to work through us in a powerful way.

Are you an encouraging person? Too often we are like Dave's friends and teammates. We cut each other down and discourage each other so much that we lose heart. But when we have even one person who believes in us, we find the strength to work hard and to reach our potential.

One person who never stops believing in us is God. Others may put us down, but our heavenly Father believes in us so much that he gave his Son to die for us.

GREAT ANSWERS BUT NO HELP

According to an ancient legend, a man became lost in his travels and wandered into a bed of quicksand.

Confucius saw the man's predicament and said, "It is evident that men should stay out of places such as this."

Next, Buddha observed the situation and said, "Let that man's plight be a lesson to the rest of the world."

Then Mohammed came by and said to the sinking man, "Alas, it is the will of God."

Finally, Jesus appeared on the scene and said, "Take my hand, brother. I will save you."

✓ APPLICATION

There are many religions in the world—and they all have things about them which are admirable and even true.

But only one provides salvation from sin. Jesus said, "I am the way, the truth and the life. No one comes to the Father but by me" (John 14:6). No other religious leader has ever made that claim—*because they can't*. Only Jesus has the power and the authority under heaven to forgive us for our sins and to give us eternal life. "For God so loved the world that he gave his one and only Son, that whoever believes in him shall not perish but have eternal life" (John 3:16).

GREAT BABIES

A group of tourists were traveling through Europe visiting historical sites. They were impressed that so many small villages were the birthplaces of great artists, poets, composers, and political leaders. While the group was strolling through a particularly picturesque village, one of the tourists approached a man who was sitting in front of a building and asked, "Excuse me, but...were any great men or women born in this village?"

The old man thought for a moment and replied, "No. Only great babies!"

☑ APPLICATION

Everyone starts off as a baby—with the opportunity to grow into greatness. This is true not only in the world, but in the kingdom of God. When we become Christians, we are "born again" as "babies in Christ." We have to grow.

Paul wrote, "Brothers, I could not address you as spiritual but as worldly—mere infants in Christ. I gave you milk, not solid food, for you were not yet ready for it. Indeed, you are still not ready" (1 Corinthians 3:2). These words were written to adult believers— yet Paul addressed them as "infants."

But we can't stay babies forever. We need to grow. The writer to the Hebrews said, "Therefore let us leave the elementary teachings about Christ and go on to maturity . . . " (Hebrews 6:1). That's why it's important to be in worship services, Sunday school, youth group, Bible studies and the like. They are opportunities for growth. The "great men and women" of the faith, just like you, started out as babies.

The Great Dane and the Alligator

There was a man who owned a Great Dane. Now this Great Dane was an extremely large and ferocious dog—definitely not the kind of dog you want jumping up in your lap. One day, as the man was walking his Great Dane down the street, he saw another man across the street who was also walking his dog—a little bitty dog with short legs no tail and no hair. It was an ugly dog and, very frankly, looked sick.

Suddenly the Great Dane saw the little ugly dog across the street and decided he hated that dog. He broke free from his owner's leash and dashed across the street on the attack. The owner of the Great Dane yelled to the man, "Look out! My dog is on the loose and he's liable to kill you and that dog of yours! You had better run!"

But the little ugly dog turned around, bared its teeth, and when the Great Dane attacked, that little dog proceeded to grab hold of the Great Dane at the foreleg and began to eat that big dog up. It ate right up the leg, right up the throat, ate its head, right down through its body, right across the tail, right down the back legs, spit out the bones, and smacked its lips—and that was the end of the Great Dane, just like that.

Well, the owner of the Great Dane was absolutely astonished by what he had just witnessed. "Man, what kind of dog is that?" the man exclaimed. "I've never in my life seen a little dog that could do something like that!"

"Dog? Dog?" the other man said. "Before he got his nose run over by a truck and his tail cut off by a train, this used to be an alligator!"

✓ APPLICATION

Appearances can be deceiving. Sometimes we judge people by how they look, but we fail to realize that on the inside, they are quite different. "Man looks at the outward appearance, but God looks at the heart" (1 Samuel 16:7).

You may feel like a puppy dog on the outside, but inside, you're an alligator. You have the power of God at your disposal to do mighty things. "I can do everything through him who gives me strength," wrote Paul (Philippians 4:13). When you are under attack by the Great Danes of the world, you can eat 'em up with the power of Christ that lives and dwells within your heart.

Haven't I Smelled You Somewhere Before?

Several years ago, Chicago newspapers carried the story of a busboy in a Chinese restaurant who went to a bank to get change for $500. The restaurant needed $250 in coins and $250 in one-dollar bills. The teller grabbed a stack of $100 bills by mistake and gave the young man $250 in coins and $25,000 in bills!

The young man noticed the error immediately, but detecting a windfall, didn't say anything. He left the bank with the money and hid it at a relative's home. With some of the money, he went to another bank and got $250 in one-dollar bills. He then returned to the restaurant, thinking he had made a small fortune.

The bank teller, when she discovered her mistake, couldn't identify the person to whom she had given the $100 bills. But she remembered how he smelled. She knew from his scent that he worked in a Chinese restaurant. She not only remembered the aroma, but she was able to connect it with the exact restaurant where the busboy worked. With the police, she located the restaurant and identified the busboy. He was promptly fired and the money was recovered. The bank decided not to prosecute, since the mistake was theirs, and they wanted to preserve good relations with the restaurant.

✓ APPLICATION

What do you smell like? As Christians, we are to carry with us "the aroma of Christ." There should be something about us that radiates the love of Christ.

Paul wrote, "For we are to God the aroma of Christ among those who are being saved and those who are perishing" (2 Corinthians 2:15). Obviously, the word "aroma" here is not to be taken literally. The aroma Paul is talking about is not necessarily detected with the nose. But it is sensed by those who come in contact with us.

Ordinarily, aroma is a byproduct of activity. When you exercise, you work up a sweat and get B.O. When you eat garlic, you get garlic breath. If you douse yourself with perfume, you smell like the fragrance counter in a department store. In the same way, when you serve Christ, and do it in a spirit of love and humility, you begin to pick up the aroma of Christ.

St. Francis of Assisi once said, "Preach the Gospel at all times; only if necessary use words." He was talking about the aroma of Christ. Can people smell you?

HELP IS ON THE WAY

One year there was a terrible flood that deluged a small midwestern town located in a valley between two rivers. Both rivers had overflowed their banks and the rains continued to fall day and night. There was no relief in sight as the town slowly but surely was being flooded. Everyone was evacuated, except for one old man who refused to leave his house—which would soon become completely submerged.

"I have faith that God will save me," the old man shouted at everyone who implored him to leave and flee to higher ground. The man believed in the power of prayer, and he trusted that God would somehow save him.

As the water covered the roads, making them impassable for cars, a man in a four-wheel-drive truck stopped at the old man's house and banged on the door. "Hurry," he cried out. "Come with me and I'll drive you to safety! You haven't much time!" But the old man continued to pray. He would not leave his house.

Within hours, the water had risen several feet, completely flooding his home. The rain continued. The old man climbed up on the kitchen table and continued to pray. As the water was lapping at his heels, a man in a rowboat paddled up to the old man's kitchen window and shouted, "Sir, get in my boat! I'll take you to safety!"

"No," the old man shouted back. "God will deliver me from this flood!"

The water got deeper and soon the old man had no choice but to climb up on his roof. The torrential rains persisted. While he was praying, he heard the chop-chop-chop of a helicopter in the sky. He looked up and saw the helicopter hovering over his house. A ladder had been lowered for him to climb.

"Go away," yelled the man at the helicopter. "You will blow me off my roof! God is going to save me! You go save someone else!"

The helicopter couldn't wait forever, so it left the old man on his rooftop, still praying. Eventually, the water engulfed the house and the old man perished in the flood.

When the old man arrived at the gates of heaven, he asked Saint Peter if he could have a talk with God. Peter took him to the throne of grace.

"Oh Lord, I prayed earnestly for the rains to stop and for your deliverance from the flood. But you left me there to drown. I don't understand!"

"My child, I heard your prayers. I sent you a four-wheel-drive truck, a rowboat, and a helicopter. Why did you send them away?"

✓ APPLICATION

God doesn't always answer our prayers in the way we expect. *But he does answer.* To have faith and trust in God means that we recognize his activity in our circumstances, regardless of how hopeless they seem. In our eyes, things may look like they are getting worse and that God has abandoned us. But God sees the big picture and we can trust that he will never leave us nor forsake us. He is at work, even when we don't realize it. "And we know that in all things God works for the good of those who love him, who have been called according to his purpose" (Romans 8:28).

We also need to remember that God works through ordinary people like you and me. Just like the rescuers in the story, when we offer help or an act of kindness to someone else, we may very well be an answer to their prayers.

THE HORSE TRADER

(You can personalize this story any way you want.)

Let's suppose that I bought a horse from a man, and for that horse I had to pay, in cold hard cash, a grand total of six dollars.

When I get home with the horse, everyone's excited. My kids think I'm a hero. And my spouse, who's a penny-pincher, thinks I'm a great bargainer. The horse is a definite hit with the family.

But after a while, problems arise. The horse is too big for the house, even though I've told the kids, "no galloping in the living room." It's getting expensive to feed this animal, too. Finally my spouse declares, "that horse has got to go." I take the horse back to the man who originally sold it to me, and he's gracious enough to buy the horse back for eight dollars.

But I miss that old horse. A lot of times at night, after the kids have gone to bed, I can be found staring up at the moon and playing my harmonica, singing cowboy songs. My spouse, bless her heart, can't stand to see me mope over old Calico, so she finally gives in and says, "Oh all right, go back and buy that horse again." This time I buy the horse from the same man for ten dollars.

You can guess what happened. No sooner did we get the horse back to the house that we began to face all the old problems again. The kids were still horsing around and the horse was doing a major number on the carpet. I could see the handwriting on the stall. I was going to have to get rid of old Calico. So, I took the horse back to the same guy and sold him my horse for twelve dollars.

I no longer have the horse, but I do have a question. After all my wheeling and dealing on that horse, did I *make money* or *lose money*? Not counting feed, or gas back and forth to the farm—did I come out ahead? Did I go in the hole? Or did I break even? And if I did gain or lose—how much did I gain or lose?

(Give the audience a chance to think about it for a minute and then ask a few volunteers to take a guess at the answer. Chances are good you will get a variety of answers—and most of them will be wrong. Have the audience vote on who they think is right.)

☑ APPLICATION

The answer is I made *four dollars*. (I spent six dollars and ten dollars = sixteen dollars; I received eight dollars and twelve dollars = twenty dollars; So, subtract sixteen dollars from twenty dollars and you get a four dollar profit.)

That problem came from a second-grade math book. It should have been real easy. But it wasn't so easy, was it? In fact it was downright confusing.

That's the way life can be sometimes. Things that seem simple sometimes aren't so simple. They can be very confusing. And it doesn't help when everybody else seems to have a different answer—and they all think they are right!

Here's the point: We are going to face all kinds of things in life that are much more difficult than a second-grade math problem. How will we know the right answer? How will we know what to do? We certainly can't afford to just guess at it. We don't want to depend on bad advice. We need to make sure that we are making the right decisions about what is right and wrong, good and bad, true and false.

That's why it's important for us to read Scripture, to pray, and to learn from those who are older and wiser than we are. That's why God gave us the church.

HOW EMBARRASSING!

A girl from the Midwest made a trip to Hollywood, California to see the sights and hopefully to catch a glimpse of a real movie star.

One afternoon, she visited Beverly Hills and went into an ice cream shop to get an ice cream cone. She put in her order and then suddenly realized that the person standing next to her at the counter was none other than Paul Newman. She couldn't believe it! Her heart leaped.

But she tried to keep her composure. She didn't want to act like an ignorant hillbilly. She didn't want to embarrass herself in front of someone like Paul Newman. So she tried not to stare or show any emotion. She paid the cashier, turned, and walked calmly out of the store.

When she got outside, she took a deep breath and suddenly realized that she had walked out of the store *without her ice cream cone.* Oh no! She must have left it on the counter. Now she was going to have to go back in and get her ice cream cone in front of Paul Newman! She just couldn't do that!

So she decided to wait outside the store until Mr. Newman had left the counter. When she noticed he was no longer there, she walked back into the store to retrieve her ice cream cone. But when she got to the counter, she felt a tap on her shoulder from behind. She turned around and . . . IT WAS PAUL NEWMAN!

Flashing his famous smile, he said, "Miss, if you're looking for your ice cream cone . . . you put it in your purse."

✓ APPLICATION

No matter how hard we try, we all end up looking pretty foolish from time to time. We can try to look "cool" or totally in control, but down deep we struggle with fears, worries, lack of confidence, low self-esteem. And sometimes we let those things drag us down and keep us from experiencing all that God wants for us.

Scripture encourages us to let go of our pride and to humble ourselves—to become a servant (which can be a pretty embarrassing thing for some people). Peter was embarrassed when he saw Jesus acting like a servant and wanting to wash his dirty feet. But think of how Jesus felt. He was God, yet he was kneeling down and doing the job of a slave.

We make look pretty foolish sometimes as Christians, but "we are fools for Christ!" (1 Corinthians 4:10).

I Ain't Lost

A man who was accustomed to giving orders and having his own way was travelling to an important meeting. He decided to take a short cut and found himself thoroughly lost. He asked the first person he saw, a young child, for directions.

"Boy, which way to Dover?" he gruffly asked.

"I don't know," the child responded, a little embarrassed.

"Well, then," the man demanded, "How far to Brighton?"

"I don't know that either," the child answered.

"Is there someone around here who can give me directions, then?" the man raised his voice.

"I don't know," shrugged the child.

The man's questions got angrier as the boy kept responding with the same answer. Finally the man lost his temper and shouted, "Well you don't know much, do you!"

Then for the first time, the boy smiled. Looking up the winding road to a little house where the evening light glowed through the window and where his brothers and sisters played in the yard, the boy said, "No . . . But I ain't lost!"

☑ APPLICATION

There are a lot of things we don't know. But if we have faith in Christ, we aren't lost. Paul wrote in 1 Corinthians 13, "Now we see but a poor reflection in a mirror; then we shall see face to face. Now I know in part; then I shall know fully . . . " Life is a mystery for us right now, and we have many unanswered questions. "We are . . . perplexed, but not in despair," Paul also wrote in 2 Corinthians 4:8. Even though we don't know everything, we aren't discouraged or feeling lost. Someday, when we see Christ, everything will become clear. Meanwhile, we can relax—knowing that God is in control. We have purpose and direction in life that comes from him.

INSIDE THE FENCE

William Barclay has written about a group of soldiers during World War II who had lost a friend in battle and wanted to give their fallen comrade a decent burial. So they found a church with a graveyard behind it, surrounded by a white fence. They found the parish priest and asked if their friend could be buried there in the church graveyard.

"Was he Catholic?" the priest inquired.

"No he was not," answered the soldiers.

"I'm sorry, then," said the priest. "Our graveyard is reserved for members of the holy church. But you can bury your friend outside the fence. I will see that the gravesite is cared for."

"Thank you, Father," said the soldiers, and they proceeded to bury their friend just outside the graveyard on the other side of the fence.

When the war had finally ended, before the soldiers returned home, they decided to visit the gravesite of their friend. They remembered the location of the church—and the grave, just outside the fence. They searched for it, but couldn't find it. Finally, they went to the priest to inquire as to its location.

"Sir, we cannot find our friend's grave," said the soldiers to the priest.

"Well," answered the priest. "After you buried your fallen friend, it just didn't seem right to me that he should be buried there, outside the fence."

"So you moved his grave?" asked the soldiers.

"No," said the priest. "I moved the fence."

✓ APPLICATION

That is exactly what God has done for us. We don't deserve a place "inside the fence." We don't deserve to go to heaven when we die. But God has graciously moved the fence. He sent his Son, Jesus Christ, to die for us so that we could be included in his forever family. "Now we have peace with God through our Lord Jesus Christ, through whom we have gained access by faith" (Romans 5:1-2).

JESUS' FAMILY TREE

(The following should be read to the group as if you are reading Scripture. It is an annotated version of Matthew, chapter 1, the genealogy of Jesus Christ. Introduce it by saying, "I want to read to you one of the most boring passages in the Bible. But I want you to help me. I'll give you hand signals along the way and I want you to respond according to the sign I give you. For example, if I give you a thumbs up sign, I want you to clap and cheer. If I give you a thumbs down sign, I want you to boo and hiss. If I give you a fist, then you say 'HUH?' Got it?" Practice this with the group a time or two, then read the passage, giving the hand signals according to the instructions below.)

↑ = thumbs up (clap and cheer)
↓ = thumbs down (boo and hiss)
✳ = fist (HUH?)

This is the list of the ancestors of Jesus Christ ↑ , a descendant of David ↑ , who was a descendant of Abraham ↑ .

Abraham was the father of Isaac ↑ , who was the father of Jacob—the man who stole his brother's birthright ↓ .

And Jacob was the father of Judah and his brothers who sold Joseph into slavery ↓ .

And Judah was the father of Perez and Zerah ✳ by Tamar ✳ and Perez was the father of Hezron and Hezron the father of Ram and Ram the father of Amminidab. ✳

And Amminidab was the father of Nahshon, who was the father of Salmon who was the father of Boaz by Rahab, the prostitute ↓ .

And Boaz was the father of Obed by Ruth, a great woman whose story is told in a book of the Bible bearing her name ↑ .

And Obed was the father of Jesse, who was the father of David the King ↑ .

And David was the father of Solomon by the wife of Uriah whom he had murdered ↓ .

And Solomon was the father of Rehoboam, a good king ↑ , but one who disobeyed God for several years ↓ .

And Rehoboam was the father of Abijah, who had fourteen wives ✳ .

And Abijah was the father of Asa, a good king but later disobeyed God and died of gangrene of the feet ↓ .

Asa was the father of Jehosophat, a king who ruled wisely most of the time ↑ .

Jehosophat was the father of Joram ✳ , the father of Uzziah, whose pride caused his downfall ↓ .

But Uzziah was the father of Jotham, a very good king in every way ↑ .

And Jotham was the father of Ahaz, a very bad king in every way ↓ .

And Ahaz was the father of Hezekiah, who cleansed the temple and re-established the kingdom ↑ .

Hezekiah was the father of Manasseh, who ruled for fifty-five years ↑ but who was evil for most of that time ↓.

Manasseh was the father of Josiah, who did right in the eyes of the Lord ↑.

Josiah was the father of Jechoniah ✳, who was the father of Shealtiel ✳, the father of Zerubbabel, a governor of the people who was chosen by God ↑.

And Zerubabbel was the father of Abiud ✳, who was the father of Eliakim ✳, the father of Azor ✳, the father of Zadok ✳, the father of Achim ✳, the father of Eliud ✳, the father of Eleazar ✳, the father of Matthan ✳, the father of Jacob (not the one we spoke of earlier) ✳.

And that Jacob was the father of Joseph the carpenter ↑, who was the husband of the Virgin Mary ↑, of whom was born Jesus, whom we call *Lord of Lords and King of Kings—the Christ!* ↑

✓ APPLICATION

The Bible is not afraid to show that there are all kinds of people in Jesus' family tree. There are good people, bad people, and people we know practically nothing about. Some were kings and heroes of the faith who were dedicated completely to God. Others, however, were sinners on a grand scale: murderers, prostitutes, and all kinds of unsavory characters. The vast majority were ordinary people, just like you and I.

This is a very hopeful thing for us. First, it means that even though our parents aren't perfect, God can still use us. Over and over in Scripture, we see bad parents producing good kids. Just because your parents or grandparents weren't faithful to God doesn't mean that you can't be.

Second, it means that God can use anybody to accomplish his will and to make a difference in the world. God didn't pick the best people in the world to produce the Messiah. Instead, he had a habit of picking people with flaws.

So, if you feel flawed—that's okay. In fact, that's even better. God wants people who will depend on him and to be strong where they are weak. God wants to use you in a powerful way. Are you willing?

Jimmy and the Genie

Once upon a time there was a boy named Jimmy who was walking in the desert and he found a magic lantern on a pile of rocks. Jimmy thought to himself, "Maybe if I rub this lantern, a genie will come out and grant me three wishes!" He tried it and sure enough, a genie appeared. Jimmy was real excited and asked the genie for three wishes.

But the genie replied, "I'm not that kind of genie. I give advice."

"Oh," said Jimmy, "then give me some advice."

"Pick up as many rocks as you can and take them home with you," said the genie, just before he disappeared.

"This is stupid," said Jimmy. "I have a long way to go and these rocks are heavy. I'm not going to pick up any rocks!" He did pick up one small rock, however, and stuck it in his pocket.

When he finally got home, Jimmy took off his dirty clothes to be washed. His mother went through his pockets and found the rock. After examining it closely, she asked Jimmy where he got that rock. Jimmy replied, "Oh, some stupid genie told me to pick up a bunch of them, but I only picked up one."

"Jimmy!" his mother cried. "This isn't a rock. This is a huge diamond! It's worth thousands of dollars!"

Unfortunately, Jimmy was never able to find that pile of rocks again.

☑ APPLICATION

There are many things in life that seem like rocks, but in reality, they are diamonds. The classes you take in school, for example. They are a drudgery and seem like a waste of time. But someday those classes, and the education that you get, will become extremely valuable to you.

And following Christ is the same way. When we serve Jesus, a lot of what we do hardly seems worth the time and effort. Sometimes being obedient to Christ is hard and may even require pain and suffering. But it's worth it. We not only are blessed by God now, but someday—when we see Jesus—those rocks become diamonds in our heavenly crowns (1 Corinthians 9:25).

JUMP!

A family was awakened by their smoke detector in the middle of the night to discover that their house was on fire. The father ran into the upstairs bedroom of his children and carried his eighteen-month-old baby in his arms while dragging his four-year-old son by the hand.

They were halfway down the stairs when the little boy remembered that he had left his teddy bear in the bedroom, so he broke free from his father's hand and ran back to the bedroom to retrieve it. In the furor and confusion, the father didn't notice that his son wasn't with him until he got outside. By now the little boy was trapped by the flames and smoke in his second-story bedroom. Smoke swirled around him and he coughed and cried out from the upstairs window, "Daddy, Daddy! Help me!"

His father yelled from below, "Jump out of the window, Andy! I'll catch you!"

In the darkness and smoke, the little boy yelled back, "But Daddy! I can't see you!"

Daddy shouted back, "That's okay, son. I can see you! Jump!"

✓ APPLICATION

There is a true saying that goes, "I don't know what the future holds, but I do know who holds the future." Do you worry about the future? Are you afraid of what you can't see? Does it seem dark and smoky? None of us can see what lies ahead, but God tells us to trust him and "jump!"

JUST A HYPHEN

Some time ago a newspaper headline read, "MISSING HYPHEN BLAMED IN ROCKET FAILURE."

It was hard to believe that a small hyphen in a computer readout caused the destruction of a huge, powerful missile.

Perhaps you've heard the old proverb: "For want of a nail a horseshoe was lost; for want of a horseshoe, a rider was lost; for want of a rider, a battle was lost; for want of a battle, a war was lost." The loss of the war, in other words, was connected to the loss of a nail.

Apparently, that was the case here. On the day in question, a Venus space probe launch vehicle, boosted by an eighteen-million-dollar U.S. Atlas rocket, was lost because a hyphen was missing from a computer equation.

Richard Morrison, a NASA official, told the House Space Committee investigating the incident that the missing hyphen caused a mathematical miscue.

Said Morrison, "The hyphen gives a cue for the spacecraft to ignore the data the computer feeds it until radar contact is once again restored. When that hyphen is left out, false information is fed into the spacecraft control systems. In this case, the computer fed in hard left, nose down and the vehicle obeyed." Who left out the hyphen? Morrison either didn't know or wasn't saying, but he speculated that it was the mistake of some senior official with advanced degrees and a Ph.D. in celestial navigation.

✓ APPLICATION

There is an important hyphen that belongs in your life, too. It doesn't seem like much, but without it, you can crash. That hyphen is *time alone with God*. A time to pray, a time to read God's Word, a time to listen to God's voice. Just a few minutes a day is all it takes to keep our lives on course.

THE KEEPER OF THE SPRING

This story has been attributed to the late Peter Marshall, former chaplain of the United States Senate.

There was once an old man who lived high above an Austrian village along the eastern slopes of the Alps. He had been hired by the village council many years ago to clear away the debris from the pools of water up in the mountain crevices that fed the lovely stream flowing through their village. With faithful, silent regularity, he patrolled the hills, removed the leaves and branches, and wiped away the silt that would otherwise choke and contaminate the fresh flow of water. By and by, the village became a popular attraction for visitors. Graceful swans floated along the crystal clear stream; picnickers gathered along its banks; and the view of the water from local shops and cafes was picturesque beyond description.

Years passed. One evening the council met for its semiannual meeting. As they reviewed the budget, they noticed a small amount that was being paid to the "keeper of the spring." The village treasurer asked, "Who is this 'keeper of the spring'? Why do we keep him on the payroll year after year? No one ever sees him. Have any of you ever met this man? For all we know, he is simply taking our money and doing us no good whatsoever. In my opinion, this person is no longer necessary."

Everyone agreed with the treasurer and the council voted unanimously to dismiss the old man.

For several weeks, nothing much changed. The village went about with its business as usual. But by autumn, the trees began to shed their leaves. Small branches snapped off and fell into the pools that fed the stream, hindering the rushing flow of sparkling water. One afternoon, someone noticed a slight yellowish-brown tint in the water. A couple days later the water was much darker. Within another week or two, a slimy film covered sections of the water along the banks and a foul odor was soon detected. The swans left the village, as did the tourists. The economy of the village was in serious peril. Likewise was the health of the village, as many were getting sick from drinking the water.

An emergency meeting of the village council was held. After much discussion, they realized their error in judgment and they hired back the old "keeper of the spring." And within a few weeks, the beautiful stream came back to life. The swans and visitors gradually returned, as did the vitality and well being of the little village in the Alps.

(From *Improving Your Serve* by Charles Swindoll, Dallas: Word, 1981)

✓ APPLICATION

What the "keeper of the spring" meant to the little village, we Christians mean to the world. Jesus called us "salt," which is to say that we are "preservers" of what is good and true in the world. Like the old man in the mountains, we are called to serve—and to be faithful. We may not get a lot of recognition or appreciation for our efforts, but we have the power to change the world. That's what Jesus wants us to do. He put us here to serve, and in a very real sense, the well-being of the whole world is dependent upon us. We do make a difference!

The "keeper of the spring" had a job which seemed to the village council very insignificant. Yet, when he was no longer around, the entire village suffered. In the same way, we are all important to the church, which is the body of Christ: "The eye cannot say to the hand, 'I don't need you!' And the head cannot say to the feet, 'I don't need you!' On the contrary, those parts of the body that seem to be weaker are indispensable—and the parts that we think are less honorable we treat with special honor" (1 Corinthians 12:21-23).

THE KING'S DRIVER

Once upon a time, there was king who lived on a great mountain. All his loyal subjects lived in the valley below. The only access to the palace at the top of the mountain was a steep, treacherous road that circled the outside of the mountain. The king loved his subjects and they also loved him, so he would visit his subjects daily. The trip was very dangerous down the mountain and the king had a trusted man to drive his chariot.

One day, the driver died and an edict went out to all the kingdom that the king needed a new driver for his chariot. There would be a contest to prove the most worthy man.

The day arrived and three men came to show their worthiness as the king's trusted driver. The first man jumped into the chariot and started down the mountain in a flash, taking the curves very swiftly and skillfully, coming within a foot of the edge of the cliffs at times, but reaching the bottom in very good time. As he reached the bottom of the mountain, the people cheered wildly and said, "This is the man! This is the man!"

The next driver cracked his whip and sped off down the mountain even faster than the first. The chariot seemed to fly as it sped down the mountain, narrowly averting disaster, but making it safely to the bottom of the mountain in record time. The crowd cheered louder still, saying "This is the man! This is the man!"

The third driver jumped into the chariot and with a steady hand, started down the steep, winding road. The crowd anticipated an even faster, more breath-taking ride. But this driver stayed close to the mountain, away from the sheer cliffs, taking each turn in the road carefully and confidently. As he reached the bottom of the mountain, the crowd was disappointed and silent. But the king said, "This is the man! This is the man!"

✓ APPLICATION

The crowd was shocked by the king's choice, but the king knew that it was better to have as his driver someone who would choose to stay close to the mountain and its safety, rather than to risk his life and the life of his king unnecessarily.

Sometimes we are like the first two drivers. We get as close as we can to the "edge" of the world (music, dress, dating, attitudes) without realizing that we are putting ourselves and others at great risk. We need to stay close to God and his safety.

THE LANTERN

Years ago in a small midwestern town one man's job was to watch the railroad crossing. When a train would approach at night he was to wave a lantern to warn those driving on the narrow road that a train was approaching and to stop until it passed by.

One particular night the train was coming down the tracks as usual and the man took his place to warn any oncoming cars. He could see a car in the distance approaching the railroad tracks so he began to wave his lantern in the moonlit sky. The car continued to come so the man waved the lantern even more briskly. The train was only seconds away from the crossing. The car was not even slowing down. The man could not believe it so he waved the lantern even harder. Still the car came. The car was almost to the track and the train was about to pass. The man could not stand in the middle of the road any longer. Again he frantically waved his lantern and the car continued to come at full speed. Finally the man jumped out of the way as the car sped by and was hit by the train on the tracks. Everyone in the car was killed.

At the investigation the grief-stricken man explained to the authorities how he tried to warn the oncoming vehicle but it would not stop. The officer in charge said to the man at the crossing, "Sir, you waved your lantern—but you forgot to light it."

✓ APPLICATION

Jesus has called us to be lights to the world. It is our job to take the good news of the Gospel to everyone we can. But it does no good to tell people about Jesus if the light within us is not shining. Without the light of Christ, we will have little impact.

LIFE INSIDE THE WOMB

Once upon a time, twin boys were conceived in the womb. Seconds, minutes, hours passed as the two embryonic lives developed. The spark of life grew and each tiny brain began to take shape and form. With the development of their brain came feeling, and with feeling, perception—a perception of surroundings, of each other, and their own lives. They discovered that life was good, and they laughed and rejoiced in their hearts.

One said to the other, "We are sure lucky to have been conceived and to have this wonderful world."

The other chimed in, "Yes, blessed be our mother who gave us life and each other."

Each of the twins continued to grow and soon their arms and fingers, legs and toes began to take shape. They stretched their bodies and churned and turned in their little world. They explored it and found the life cord which gave them life from their mother's blood. They were grateful for this new discovery and sang, "How great is the love of our mother—that she shares all she has with us!"

Weeks passed into months and with the advent of each new month, they noticed a change in each other and in themselves.

"We are changing," one said. "What can it mean?"

"It means," said the other, "that we are drawing near to birth."

An unsettling chill crept over the two. They were afraid of birth, for they knew that it meant leaving their wonderful world behind.

Said the one, "Were it up to me, I would live here forever."

"But we must be born," said the other. "It has happened to all the others." Indeed, there was evidence inside the womb that the mother had carried life before theirs. "And I believe that there is life after birth, don't you?"

"How can there be life after birth?" cried the one. "Do we not shed our life cord and also the blood tissue when we are born? And have you ever talked to anyone that has been born? Has anyone ever re-entered the womb after birth to describe what birth is like? NO!" As he spoke, he fell into despair, and in his despair he moaned, "If the purpose of conception and our growth inside the womb is to end in birth, then truly our life is senseless." He clutched his precious life cord to his breast and said, "And if this is so, and life is absurd, then there really can be no mother!"

"But there is a mother," protested the other. "Who else gave us nourishment? Who else created this world for us?"

"We get our nourishment from this cord—and our world has always been here!" said the one. "And if there is a mother—where is she? Have you ever seen her? Does she ever talk to you? NO! We invented the mother when we were young because it satisfied a need in us. It made us feel secure and happy."

Thus, while the one raved and despaired, the other resigned himself to birth and placed his trust in the hands of his mother. Hours turned into days, and days into weeks. And soon it was time. They both knew their birth was at hand, and they both feared what they did not know. As the one was first to be conceived, so he was the first to be born, the other following.

They cried as they were born into the light. They coughed out fluid and gasped the dry air. And when they were sure they had been born, they opened their eyes—seeing life after birth for the very first time. What they saw was the beautiful eyes of their mother, as they were cradled lovingly in her arms. They were home.

☑ APPLICATION

"No eye has seen, no ear has heard, no mind has conceived what God has prepared for those who love him" (1 Corinthians 2:9).

THE LIFESAVING STATION

On a dangerous seacoast where shipwrecks often occur, there was once a crude little lifesaving station. The building was just a hut, and there was only one boat. But the few, devoted members kept a constant watch over the sea, and with no thought for their own safety, went out day and night tirelessly searching for the lost.

Some of the people who were saved, and various others in the surrounding community, wanted to become associated with the lifesaving station and to give of their time and money for the support of its work. New boats were bought and new crews were trained. The little lifesaving station grew.

Some of the members of the life-saving station were unhappy that the building was so small and so poorly equipped. They felt that a more comfortable place should be provided for those who were being saved from the sea. They replaced the emergency cots with beds and put better furniture in the enlarged building. Now the lifesaving station became a popular gathering place for its members, and they decorated it beautifully and furnished it exquisitely. It became sort of a club.

Fewer members were now interested in going to sea on lifesaving missions so they hired professional lifeboat crews who were specially trained to save lives. The lifesaving motif still prevailed, and a ceremonial lifeboat was placed in the room in honor of all those people who had been saved in the past.

About that time, a large ship was wrecked off the coast, and the hired crews brought in boatloads of cold, wet and half-drowned people. They were dirty and sick and some of them were from a foreign country and couldn't speak their language. The beautiful new club was in chaos. So the property committee of the lifesaving station called an emergency meeting and decided to build a shower house outside the club where victims of shipwrecks could be cleaned up and properly instructed regarding the rules of the lifesaving station.

At the next meeting, there was a split in the club's membership. Most of the members wanted to stop the club's lifesaving activities because they were unpleasant and a hindrance to the normal social life of the club. Other members, however, insisted that lifesaving was the primary purpose of the club. They pointed out that they were still called a "lifesaving station." But they were finally voted down and told that if they wanted to save lives, then they could start their own lifesaving station down the coast. They did.

As the years went by, the new lifesaving station experienced the same changes that had occurred with the old. It evolved into a club, and yet another life-saving station was founded. History continued to repeat itself, and if you visit the sea coast today, you will find a number of exclusive clubs along that shore.

Shipwrecks are frequent in those waters, but most of the people drown.

(From *Ideas #6*, Youth Specialties©1978)

✓ APPLICATION

Jesus established his church to be a life-saving station. His final instructions to the church are found in Matthew 28:19-20: "Therefore go and make disciples of all nations, baptizing them in the name of the Father and of the Son and of the Holy Spirit, and teaching them to obey everything I have commanded you . . . ". Our job is to go out into the world and rescue the perishing. It's not just the job of a few professional life-savers. It's our job, too.

THE LOGIC EXAM

In a beginning logic course at a major university, the professor made an unusual offer to his students who were preparing for their final exam. He told them, "You can bring to class on the day of the exam as much information as you can fit onto one piece of notebook paper."

So every student sharpened his or her pencils and worked all week trying to cram as many facts as possible onto an 8 1/2 x 11 inch sheet of notebook paper.

But one student walked into the class, put a piece of notebook paper on the floor, and had an advanced logic student stand on the paper. The advanced logic student told him everything he needed to know. As a result, he was the only student in the class to receive an A.

✓ APPLICATION

The ultimate final exam will come when you have to stand before God and he asks, "Why should I give you eternal life?" On your own, you cannot pass that exam. No matter how much you know, you don't have the right answer to that question.

But we have someone who will stand in for us and answer correctly. His name is Jesus.

When Jesus died for our sins, he took the F that we deserve so that we could get an A. Jesus went to the cross to die for our sins, and that allows us to stand before God with a perfect score. As the apostle John wrote, "We have one who speaks to the Father in our defense—Jesus Christ, the Righteous One. He is the atoning sacrifice for our sins, and not only for ours but also for the sins of the whole world" (1 John 2:1-2).

Lost and Found

When she turned twenty-one, Tammy Harris from Roanoke, Virginia, began searching for her biological mother. After a year, she had not succeeded. What she didn't know was that her mother, Joyce Schultz, had been trying to locate her for twenty years.

According to the story that appeared in newspapers all over the country, there was one more thing that Tammy didn't know. Her mother was one of her co-workers at the convenience store where she worked! One day, Joyce overheard Tammy talking with another co-worker about trying to find her mother. Soon they were comparing birth certificates. When Tammy realized that the co-worker she had known was in fact her mother, she fell into her arms. "We held on for the longest time," Tammy said. "It was the best day of my life!"

✓ APPLICATION

Maybe you are like Tammy Harris. You've been searching for someone or something that has been missing in your life. You've been trying to find someone or something to give you meaning and purpose—or a sense of belonging—or happiness—or love.

What you may not have realized is that someone has also been searching for you—and he is closer than you think. God has been close to you all the time, and he is waiting for you to make the discovery that he is *your* heavenly Father, who loves you and wants to have a close relationship with you. All you have to do is fall into his arms. And when you do—it will be the best day of your life!

Love and the Cabbie

Columnist Art Buchwald tells the story of a day when he was riding in a cab in New York City with a friend. When they got out of the cab, the friend said to the driver, "Thank you for the ride. You did a superb job of driving this cab!"

The taxi driver seemed stunned for a second and said, "Are you a wise guy or something?"

"No," said the man, "I'm serious. I admire the way you keep cool in heavy traffic. Not many cab drivers are able to do that. I'm glad I rode in your cab today!"

"Yeah, sure," said the cab driver and he drove off.

Buchwald asked his friend, "What was that all about?"

"I am trying to bring love back to New York City," said the man. "I believe it's the only thing that can save the city."

"You think one man can save New York City?"

"It's not one man," said the man. "I believe I have made that taxi driver's day. Suppose he has twenty fares. He's going to be nice to those twenty fares because someone was nice to him. Those fares will in turn be kinder to their employees, shopkeepers or waiters, or even their own families. Eventually, the goodwill could spread to at least a thousand people. Now that isn't bad, is it?"

"But you are depending on that taxi driver to pass your goodwill on to others."

"Maybe he won't," said the man. "But I might say something nice to ten different people today. If, out of ten, I can make three happy, then I can indirectly influence the attitudes of three thousand or more."

"You're some kind of a nut," said Buchwald to his friend.

"That shows how cynical you've become," said the man. "Take postal workers, for instance. The reason so many of them hate their work is because no one is telling them that they are doing a good job."

"But they aren't doing a good job."

"They're not doing a good job because they don't believe anyone cares if they do or not," replied the man.

Buchwald and his friend continued walking down the street and

noticed five workmen eating their lunch. The friend stopped and said, "That's a magnificent job you men have done. It must be difficult and dangerous work."

The workmen looked at Buchwald's friend suspiciously.

"When will this job be finished?" the friend asked.

"June," growled one of the workmen.

"Ah, that is really impressive. You must all be very proud of what you are doing here!"

As they walked away, Buchwald said, "I still don't think you are doing any good."

"On the contrary," said the man, "when those workmen digest my words, they'll feel better about what they are doing and somehow the city will benefit."

"But you can't do this alone," said Buchwald. "You're just one man."

"But I'm not discouraged," he said. "I'm hoping to enlist others in my campaign."

They continued walking down the street.

"You just smiled at a very plain-looking woman," Buchwald said to his friend.

"Yes, I know," the man replied. "And if she's a schoolteacher, her class is going to be in for a fantastic day."

☑ APPLICATION

Most of us don't realize the impact that we can have on the world by sharing God's love one person at a time. When we do, we can set off a chain reaction that will reap huge dividends for the kingdom of God. You can make a big difference in the world with seemingly insignificant acts of kindness. Just as Jesus took a few loaves and fishes beside the sea of Galilee and fed a multitude, God is able to take the small things we do for him and perform miracles in other people's lives. Try it and see what happens!

MAKE ME LIKE JOE

    A drunk was miraculously converted at a Bowery mission. Prior to his conversion, Joe had gained the reputation of being a dirty wino for whom there was no hope, only a miserable existence in the ghetto. But following his conversion to a new life with God, everything changed. Joe became the most caring person that anyone associated with the mission had ever known. Joe spent his days and nights hanging out at the mission doing whatever needed to be done. There was never any task that was too lowly for Joe to take on. There was never anything that he was asked to do that he considered beneath him. Whether it was cleaning up the vomit left by some violently sick alcoholic or scrubbing the toilets after careless men left the bathroom filthy, Joe did what was asked with a soft smile on his face and with a seeming gratitude for the chance to help. He could be counted on to feed feeble men who wandered into the mission off the street, and to undress and tuck into bed men who were too out of it to take care of themselves.

    One evening, when the director of the mission was delivering his evening evangelistic message to the usual crowd of still and sullen men with drooped heads, there was one man who looked up, came down the aisle to the altar and knelt to pray, crying out for God to help him to change. The repentant drunk kept shouting, "Oh God, make me like Joe! Make me like Joe! Make me like Joe! Make me like Joe!"

The director of the mission leaned over and said to the man, "Son, I think it would be better if you prayed, 'Make me like *Jesus*!'"

The man looked up at the director with a quizzical expression on his face and asked, "Is he like Joe?"

(From *Everything You've Heard is Wrong* by Tony Campolo, Dallas: Word, 1992, pg. 73)

✓ APPLICATION

The first real communication of anything spiritual usually comes through people who demonstrate loving humility in the regular turn of daily events and especially in the rough spots of life. When we share the humble spirit of Christ in the workplace, at school, at home, or wherever we are, we do more to point people to Christ than any kind of preaching or evangelistic technique. Our goal is to let people see Jesus in us, to be a reflection of him. Someone has said, "You may be the only Jesus a person ever sees." What do they see? Let us be an accurate reflection of Jesus, who "being in very nature God, did not consider equality with God something to be grasped, but made himself nothing, taking the very nature of a servant . . . " (Philippians 2:6-7).

MEDICAL TERMS YOU NEED TO KNOW

With so many hospital and doctor shows on TV these days, it's important to have a good understanding of medical terminology. Here are a few definitions that will help you know what's going on when they start talking medical talk on TV.

1. Artery   The study of painting
2. Bacteria   The back door of the cafeteria
3. Barium   What doctors do when their patients die
4. Bowel   A letter like A, E, I, O or U
5. Caesarean Section   A neighborhood in Rome
6. CAT Scan   Searching for a kitty
7. Cauterize   To make eye contact with a girl
8. Coma   A punctuation mark
9. Enema   Someone who is not your friend
10. Fester   Quicker
11. Fibula   A small lie
12. Labor Pain   When you get hurt at work

13.	Nitrates	Cheaper than day rates
14.	Node	Was aware of
15.	Outpatient	A patient who fainted
16.	Pelvis	An Elvis impersonator
17.	Recovery Room	A place to do upholstery
18.	Rectum	Almost killed 'em
19.	Secretion	Something you don't want anyone to know
20.	Seizure	A Roman emperor
21.	Tablet	A small table
22.	Terminal	Where the planes land
23.	Urine	Opposite of "you're out"
24.	Varicose	Nearby
25.	Vein	To be conceited

✓ APPLICATION

In reality, most of us don't know much about the medical profession. We watch it on TV and admire the doctors and nurses who seem to know what they are doing. Perhaps what makes those shows so glamorous and exciting is that we can't do what they do. The doctors on those shows seem almost superhuman, like miracle workers.

But real doctors and real hospitals aren't very glamorous. They are actually rather sterile places full of sick people. TV makes a hospital room look like a place of romance and suspense, when actually it is just a place where people feel really bad, and doctors often don't know what they are doing.

Still, we wish we could be as intelligent and heroic as the doctors we see on TV. We wish we could touch people they way they do and save lives. And we can. Whenever we share Jesus Christ with another person, or listen to them share a need with us so that we can pray for them, or offer an act of kindness—we are, in a very real sense, lifesavers. We have the power to bring healing to broken lives on behalf of "the Great Physician," Jesus Christ.

MELODY IN F

Feeling footloose and frisky, a featherbrained freshman from Fargo named Fred forced his father to fork over the family fortune. Feeling free, Fred flew far to fancy foreign fields—finding foolish frivolities, frequent fornication, and fabulous feasting with faithless friends.

Fred frittered away his father's fortune, fleeced by his friends in folly. Fully fatigued and facing famine, Fred found himself a feed-flinger in a filthy farmyard with fungus on his face and a fist full of fresh fragrant fertilizer. "Fooey! What a fiasco!" the frazzled fugitive forlornly fumbled, frankly facing facts. "My father's flunkies fare far finer!"

Freezing, frightened, and frustrated by failure, Fred fled forthwith to his Fargo family, filled with fear and foreboding. Falling at his father's feet, he forlornly fumbled, "Father, I've flunked, and fruitlessly forfeited family favor. Frankly, I've flopped."

Fortunately for Fred, the farsighted father said, "Fantastic!" and forgetting Fred's failings, frantically flagged the flunkies to furnish Fred with fashionable flannel, fetch a fatling from the flock, and fix a feast!

But Fred's fault-finding brother Farley flew into a fit, frowning on Fred's fancy footwork and his father's fickle forgiveness. "Fred's a fool!" said Farley. But the faithful father figured, "Filial fidelity is fine, Farley, but the fugitive is found! What forbids fervent festivity? Let flags be unfurled! Find the fiddles and flutes! Let fanfares flare!"

Father's forgiveness formed the foundation for Fred the former fugitive's future fortitude.

✓ **APPLICATION**

Use this as an alternate reading of Jesus' parable of the Prodigal Son, found in Luke 15.

The Mice in the Piano

Once upon a time a family of mice lived in a large piano. They loved their piano world and the music that often came to them, filling all the dark spaces with sound and harmony. At first the mice were impressed by it. They drew comfort and wonder from the thought that there was someone who made the music. Although this someone was invisible to them, he felt close to them. They loved to think about the Unseen Player whom they could not see.

Then one day a daring mouse climbed up part of the piano and returned in a very thoughtful mood. He had made a discovery which revealed how the music was made. Wires were the secret. He had found tightly stretched wires of graduated lengths which trembled and vibrated. Now the mice had to revise all their old beliefs. Only the most conservative mice could believe any longer in the Unseen Player.

Later, another mouse explorer returned from an expedition with yet a new discovery about the origins of the music. Hammers were the true secret! There were dozens of hammers that danced and leaped upon the wires! This was a more complicated theory, but it all went to show that they lived in a purely mechanical universe. The Unseen Player came to be thought of as a myth.

Meanwhile, the Unseen Player continued to play.

✓ APPLICATION

And meanwhile, God continues to love us and to take care of us.

THE MILKMAN'S GIFT

When Cheryl Prewitt was four years old, she hung around her father's small country grocery store. Almost daily, the milkman would come into the store and greet her with the words, "How's my little Miss America?" At first she giggled, but eventually she became comfortable with it . . . and even liked it a little. Soon the milkman's greeting became a childhood fantasy . . . then a teenage dream. Finally, it became a goal . . . and in 1980, she stood on a stage in Atlantic City and was crowned . . . Miss America.

✓ APPLICATION

The milkman probably never realized that his greeting to little Cheryl Prewitt would be taken seriously and one day become a reality.

In the same way, you may not realize that your words have power to influence people in a positive or a negative way. If we say encouraging things to other people, they will be more likely to live up to those words of encouragement. But if you cut someone down and say discouraging things, it may lead them to despair and negative behaviors.

"Therefore encourage one another and build each other up," wrote Paul in 1 Thessalonians 5:11. If you do, you will be giving someone a wonderful gift.

The Mud Flats

Just outside Anchorage, Alaska, there is a place called the Turn-Again Arms. This particular area has one of the fastest tide rates in the world. The tide rushes in and out at about ten feet per minute. The water is so cold that if you got caught in it you would die within a few moments. When the tide is out, there is a huge flat area of mud. It looks like a great place to ride off-road vehicles. But this area—called the mud flats—is not just mud but also glacial silt. When the tide rushes out, the water that is left settles quickly. When it settles, it leaves air pockets, and those air pockets form vacuums. You never know where they are and they are never in the same place twice. If you step in one of them, it will suck you in and you can't get out. It's not exactly like quicksand but more like superglue as it locks you in.

In the summer of 1991, a couple who had just gotten married decided to spend their honeymoon in this part of Alaska. They went out riding ATV's and decided to ride around on one particular mud flat. The bride's vehicle stalled and she jumped off to see what the problem was. She jumped into one of these areas of glacial silt and sank in up to her knees. As she struggled to get out, she sunk to her thighs. Her husband rode up on his ATV and she warned him not to get off his vehicle. People on the road above them saw what was happening and called for help,

yelling at the man not to get off his vehicle. Within moments the fire department arrived and tried to blast her out of the mud flat by using water hoses. It didn't work. Then they brought in an army helicopter from the Air Force base. They tried to pull her out with a rope and harness attached around her waist. As the helicopter pulled up her legs dislocated. They knew if they pulled any more they would have ripped her legs from her body. They tried to put a wet suit around her, thinking that when the tides came in, it would keep her warm. But they could only get the wet suit around part of her body. When the tides came in she died while her husband helplessly watched.

✓ APPLICATION

This tragic true story illustrates what sin is like. It looks so good. It is so inviting. You see it and you just want to get out there and have fun. But it turns out to be glacial silt. It sucks you in and ultimately ends up taking your life.

THE NATIVE AMERICAN AND THE CRICKET

A Native American and his friend were in downtown New York City, walking near Times Square in Manhattan. It was during the noon lunch hour and the streets were filled with people. Cars were honking their horns, taxicabs were squealing around corners, sirens were wailing, and the sounds of the city were almost deafening.

Suddenly, the Native American said, "I hear a cricket."

His friend said, "What? You must be crazy. You couldn't possibly hear a cricket in all of this noise!"

"No, I'm sure of it," the Native American said. "I heard a cricket."

"That's crazy," said the friend.

The Native American listened carefully for a moment, and then walked across the street to a big cement planter where some shrubs were growing. He looked into the bushes, beneath the branches, and sure enough, he located a small cricket. His friend was utterly amazed.

"That's incredible," said his friend. "You must have super-human ears!"

"No," said the Native American. "My ears are no different from yours. It all depends on what you're listening for."

"But that can't be!" said the friend. "I could never hear a cricket in this noise."

"Yes, it's true," came the reply. "It depends on what is really important to you. Here, let me show you."

He reached into his pocket, pulled out a few coins, and discreetly dropped them on the sidewalk. And then, with the noise of the crowded street still blaring in their ears, they noticed every head within twenty feet turn and look to see if the money that tinkled on the pavement was theirs.

"See what I mean?" asked the Native American. "It all depends on what's important to you."

✓ APPLICATION

What's important to you? What do you listen for? Some people say that there is no God, and that he never speaks to us anymore. But perhaps they can't see or hear him because they aren't listening for him. They are living for themselves, not for God.

If you are in tune with God, you will be able to notice him at work in your life and in the world. And you'll be able to hear him when he speaks.

Jesus said, "For this people's heart has become calloused; they hardly hear with their ears, and they have closed their eyes. Otherwise they might see with their eyes, hear with their ears, understand with their hearts and turn, and I would heal them . . . But blessed are your eyes because they see, and your ears because they hear" (Matthew 13:15-16).

The Native American and the Rattlesnake

There once lived a young Native American boy who felt he was ready to become a man. The chief of the tribe said, "To become a man, you must first survive in the high mountains for one week. If you survive, then you will be considered a man."

So the little boy set out for the mountains on his quest to become a man. Climbing to the highest mountain, he noticed a rattlesnake lying in a patch of snow.

The young boy was startled when the snake spoke to him. "Please help me," said the shivering snake. "I'm cold and lost, far from home. Please pick me up and carry me back to the valley where it is warm. If I stay here, I will surely die."

The boy drew close, but was careful not to get too close, because he knew that this kind of snake was very deadly. "I know your kind," said the boy. "You will only bite me when I pick you up."

The snake said, "Oh, but I won't bite you. I will be your friend if you will carry me down the mountain. You can trust me."

The boy thought it over and decided that any snake that could talk must be a special kind of snake. So he picked up the snake and carried him all the way down to the warm valley. He gently placed the snake on the ground, and immediately, the snake curled up and struck the boy on the neck.

The boy cried out with a scream, "You bit me! You promised that you wouldn't bite me. Now I'm going to die!"

With an evil hiss, the snake slithered off into the grass and said, "I can't help that. You knew exactly what I was when you picked me up. So long, sucker."

☑ APPLICATION

That's the way sin is. It tempts us and draws us close. It tells us lies. It persuades us to go against our better judgment and to handle it, not believing that it will surely kill us. But that is when sin is most deadly—when we think it is our friend.

"But each one is tempted when, by his own evil desire, he is dragged away and enticed. Then, after desire has conceived, it gives birth to sin; and sin, when it is full grown, gives birth to death" (James 1:14,15).

THE NEW GORILLA

A man was looking for a job and he noticed that there was an opening at the local zoo. He inquired about the job and discovered that the zoo had a very unusual position that they wanted to fill. Apparently their gorilla had died, and until they could get a new one, they needed someone to dress up in a gorilla suit and act like a gorilla for a few days. He was to just sit, eat and sleep. His identity would be kept a secret, of course. Thanks to a very fine gorilla suit, no one would be the wiser.

The zoo offered good pay for this job, so the man decided to do it. He tried on the suit and sure enough, he looked just like a gorilla. They led him to the cage; he took a position at the back of the cage and pretended to sleep. But after a while, he got tired of sitting, so he walked around a little bit, jumped up and down and tried a few gorilla noises. The people who were watching him seemed to really like that. When he would move or jump around, they would clap and cheer and throw him peanuts. And the man loved peanuts. So he jumped around some more and tried climbing a tree. That seemed to really get the crowd excited. They threw more peanuts. Playing to the crowd, he grabbed a vine and swung from one side of the cage to the other. The people loved it and threw more peanuts. Wow, this is great, he thought. He swung higher and the crowd grew bigger. He continued to swing on the vine, getting higher and higher—and then all of a sudden, the vine broke! He swung up and out of the cage, landing in the lion's cage that was next door.

He panicked. There was a huge lion not twenty feet away, and it looked very hungry. So the man in the gorilla suit started jumping up and down, screaming and yelling, "Help, help! Get me out of here! I'm not really a gorilla! I'm a man in a gorilla suit! Heeelllp!"

The lion quickly pounced on the man, held him down and said, "Will you SHUT UP! You're going to get both of us fired!"

☑ APPLICATION

Sooner or later we all get found out. Sooner or later we all blow our cover. It is only a matter of time before who we are and what we really are becomes obvious to everyone. Any attempt to conceal our true nature will eventually be futile. In some stressful, off-guarded moment, who and what we are will surface. There is no point in pretending. Who we are and what we are, sooner or later, says Scripture, "will be declared from the rooftops."

NOBEL'S LEGACY

The Nobel Peace Prize is the supreme award given to those who have made an exceptional contribution to the betterment of the world. Other Nobel Prizes are given to those who have made outstanding contributions in the arts and sciences. There is a story about the Nobel Prize that is rarely ever told.

Alfred Nobel, a Swedish chemist, made his fortune by inventing powerful explosives and licensing the formula to governments to make weapons. One day Nobel's brother died, and a newspaper by accident printed an obituary notice for Alfred instead of the deceased brother.

It identified him as the inventor of dynamite who made a fortune by enabling armies to achieve new levels of mass destruction. Nobel had the unique opportunity to read his own obituary in his lifetime and to see how he would be remembered. He was shocked to think that this was what his life would add up to: he would be remembered as a merchant of death and destruction.

He took his fortune and used it to establish the awards for accomplishments contributing to life rather than death. And today, Nobel indeed is remembered for his contribution to peace and human achievement—not explosives.

✓ APPLICATION

All of us have the ability to leave behind a legacy of peace and goodwill if we choose to do so. Nobel spent much of his life being "successful" in the business world—only to realize that he had made a huge mistake. Like Scrooge in Dickens' *A Christmas Carol*, Nobel got a glimpse of the future and he didn't like what he saw. So he turned his life around and gave all that he had made to make the world a better place. What are you living for? If people who know you could write your obituary, what would they write?

NOT-SO-IDENTICAL TWINS

There were once two brothers who were identical twins. Now even though they looked exactly alike, they were exact opposites when it came to their personalities. One brother was an eternal optimist—he always saw good in everything and everybody. The other brother, however, was an eternal pessimist—he never saw good in anything anywhere.

One Christmas, their parents decided to try an experiment on them to see if there was any way that the two brothers could find some balance in their personalities. To the pessimist son, the parents gave a bright, shiny bicycle. To their optimist son, they gave a bag filled with nothing but straw. They put the presents under the tree with the boys' names on them and waited to see what would happen.

On Christmas morning, the two boys ran downstairs to discover what they had received from their parents. Upon finding the bicycle, the pessimist proclaimed, "A bicycle? Why did you give me a bicycle? It's too cold to ride outside, and besides, I will probably fall and hurt myself. I can't believe you got me a lousy bicycle!"

The optimist opened his present, found the bag of straw and

thought for a minute. Suddenly he ran to the backyard and began looking around frantically. His parents and brothers were completely puzzled, and they finally asked him, "What in the world are you doing?" To which he replied, "Well, after getting that bag of straw, I just know there's a pony around here someplace! I just haven't found him yet!"

✓ APPLICATION

Attitude can make a huge difference in your circumstances. When things happen to you at home, at school, with your friends—you have two choices. You can take the high road or the low road. The high road is to remain positive and look for the good in your situation. The low road is to be negative and to see only the bad. One road leads to happiness, the other to despair. Really, the choice is yours. Circumstances don't have to control your life. You can instead control how those circumstances affect you. You have the power.

As Christians, we have every reason to take the high road and to be optimistic about life. Because of Christ, we have hope—real hope. We know that no matter what happens, God is in control and we have the victory that Christ won for us on the cross. The apostle Paul was in prison when he wrote, "Rejoice in the Lord always. I will say it again: Rejoice!" (Philippians 4:4). That's the kind of attitude we need to have.

ONE MORE YEAR

There once was a sorcerer who fell into disfavor with the king and was sentenced to death. On the day of his scheduled execution, the sorcerer told the king that if the king would allow him to live for one more year, he would make the king world-famous. The sorcerer guaranteed to make the king's horse talk, and in so doing give the king worldwide fame. If the sorcerer failed, the king could kill him and the sorcerer wouldn't object.

The king agreed to this and the sorcerer was spared for one year and placed in the palace dungeon. A duke, who was a friend of the sorcerer, sneaked into the dungeon and said, "You are indeed a fool. I know and you know that you don't have the power to make the king's horse talk. You have no hope at all of success. You will surely die!"

"But," the sorcerer replied, "I have one year to live. Many things can happen in one year. Perhaps the king will die. Or I may die. Or I may even teach a horse to talk. Regardless, I still have one more year!"

☑ APPLICATION

A lot can happen in one year. What will you do with the coming year that God has given to you?

THE ORPHAN GIRL

Once upon a time there was a little girl whose parents had died. She lived with her grandmother in an upstairs bedroom.

One night a fire broke out in the house and the grandmother perished while trying to rescue the little girl. The fire spread through the house very quickly and the first floor was soon engulfed in flames.

As the fire spread through the house, the neighbors arrived and tried to enter the house but couldn't because all the doors were blocked by flames. Someone called 911, but they knew that the fire department would arrive too late to save the little girl who was trapped upstairs. They could hear her cries in the upstairs bedroom, but there was nothing that anyone could do.

Suddenly, a man appeared with a tall ladder and raised it against the side of the house. He climbed the ladder, broke a window and disappeared into the house. Soon he reappeared at the window with the little girl in his arms. He descended the ladder just as an ambulance arrived, and he delivered the little girl to the paramedics who took her quickly to the hospital. The little girl survived, but the man who saved her disappeared into the night.

A few months later, the little girl went before a judge who had the responsibility of placing her in a foster home. She had no living relatives, so it was up to the courts to find a proper home for her.

The judge decided to interview several prospective people who were willing to take her in. After interviewing them all, he would make his decision. The little girl was present in the courtroom during all these proceedings.

The first person requesting custody of the child was a schoolteacher. She pointed out that the child would need a good education, and as a teacher, she could make sure that she learned a great deal. She knew how to deal with children, she said, and she knew how to take care of a girl like this one.

The next person was a farmer. He offered the little girl a wholesome environment, where she would learn principles of hard work and the simple life. She would get to be around animals and learn responsibility.

Next was a rich woman who said, "I can give this child anything she needs or wants. I will provide her with the finest clothes and send her to the best schools. If she lives with me, she will have whatever her heart desires."

Several other people were interviewed, each of whom explained why it would be to the little girl's advantage to live with them.

"Does anyone else have anything to say before I make my decision?" asked the judge.

Just then a man came forward from the back of the courtroom. He walked very slowly and with a slight limp. From his old clothes, it was obvious that he wasn't rich or well-educated. When he got to the front of the room, he stood directly in front of the little girl and held out his arms. The crowd gasped. His hands and his arms were terribly burned and scarred.

"This is the man who saved me!" cried the little girl. With a leap, she threw her arms around the man's neck, holding on for dear life, just as she had on the day of the fire. She buried her face in his shoulder and sobbed for a few moments. Then she looked up and smiled with a grin that lit up the courtroom.

"I think I've just made my decision," said the judge. And the court was adjourned.

✓ APPLICATION

There is an old hymn that goes "Oh, how I love Jesus . . . Because he first loved me." When we come to Jesus Christ, we come to him out of gratitude for what he did for us on the cross. We live for Jesus because of what he has done for us.

THE PAINTING IN THE WAREHOUSE

As owner of the world's most influential newspaper, William Randolph Hearst was a very rich and powerful man. He was also an art collector. He loved beautiful paintings.

One day, Mr. Hearst saw a picture of two particularly exquisite works of art and decided that he just had to have them for his personal collection. He summoned one of his staff members and told him to mount a search to find out where those paintings were located and to purchase them, regardless of the cost.

His staff spent weeks travelling, writing letters, and making phone calls to locate the two paintings. Finally they were found—in a warehouse on the other side of town in the very city in which Hearst operated his newspaper.

Hearst was filled with anticipation as his staff led him to the warehouse where the paintings were located. When they arrived at the warehouse, Hearst was suddenly confused.

"*This* is where the paintings are located?" he asked incredulously.

"Yes," responded his staff member. "Is something wrong?"

"Well, I already own this warehouse and everything in it!" he said. "Those paintings have been mine all along!"

✓ APPLICATION

You can spend your entire life looking for that "certain something" that will give you happiness and fulfillment. But all you need to do is look in your own backyard. God has given you a precious gift which is yours for the taking—a relationship with Jesus Christ. All you have to do is receive him.

Alternate application: Have you ever felt like you were a nobody, a person who would never amount to anything? When you are feeling that way, it's easy to look with envy at other people who are more talented, more gifted, better looking, and feel bad about yourself. But it's likely that you haven't checked out the "painting in the warehouse." God has given you talents and abilities that you probably don't even realize you have. The key is to discover them and to use them.

PALM MONDAY

The donkey awakened, his mind still savoring the afterglow of the most exciting day of his life. Never before had he felt such a rush of pleasure and pride.

He walked into town and found a group of people by the well. "I'll show myself to them," he thought.

But they didn't notice him. They went on drawing their water and paid him no mind.

"Throw your garments down," he said crossly. "Don't you know who I am?"

They just looked at him in amazement. Someone slapped him across the tail and ordered him to move.

"Miserable heathens!" he muttered to himself. "I'll just go to the market where the good people are. They will remember me."

But the same thing happened. No one paid any attention to the donkey as he strutted down the main street in front of the market place.

"The palm branches! Where are the palm branches!" he shouted. "Yesterday, you threw palm branches!"

Hurt and confused, the donkey returned home to his mother.

"Foolish child," she said gently. "Don't you realize that without him, you are just an ordinary donkey?"

✓ APPLICATION

Just like the donkey who carried Jesus in Jerusalem, we are most fulfilled when we are in the service of Jesus Christ. Without him, all our best efforts are like "filthy rags" (Isaiah 64:6) and amount to nothing. When we lift up Christ, however, we are no longer ordinary people but key players in God's plan to redeem the world.

PHAMOUS PHOBIAS

Psychologists have given names to almost every fear (or phobia) under the sun. For example, if you have a fear of . . .

    . . . crowds—then you have *ochlophobia.*
    . . . darkness—you have *nyctophobia.*
    . . . being looked at by other people—you have *scopophobia.*
    . . . failure—you have *kakorrhaphiophobia.*
    . . . loneliness—you have *monophobia.*
    . . . marriage—you have *gamophobia.*
    . . . poverty—you have *peniaphobia.*
    . . . responsibility—you have *hypengyophobia.*
    . . . ridicule (being made fun of)—you have *categelophobia.*
    . . . school—yep, you guessed it, *schoolphobia.*
    . . . God—*theophobia.*
    . . . Death—*thanataphobia.*
    . . . Hell—*hadephobia.*

✓ APPLICATION

What are you afraid of? We all have fears—some that are good (they protect us) and some that are bad (they destroy us). If you are a person with too many fears, your life will not only be miserable, but you are an easy target for Satan. The world preys on your fears—your fear of rejection, your fear of growing old, your fear of pain, your fear of loneliness.

But Jesus taught that we shouldn't be afraid of anyone or anything that would hurt us in the physical realm. God will take care of all our needs. We really don't have to worry. On the other hand, Jesus said, we should fear anyone or anything that could hurt us spiritually and separate us from eternal life (Matthew 10:28).

But for the Christian, God has taken care of that, too. As Paul wrote, "For I am convinced that neither death nor life, neither angels nor demons, neither the present nor the future, nor any powers, neither height nor depth, nor anything else in all creation, will be able to separate us from the love of God that is in Christ Jesus our Lord" (Romans 8:38-9). We have nothing to fear.

The President and the Little Boy

During the war between the states, a young soldier in the Union Army lost his older brother and his father in the battle of Gettysburg. The soldier decided to go to Washington, D.C. to see President Lincoln to ask for an exemption from military service so that he could go back and help his sister and mother with the spring planting on the farm. When he arrived in Washington, after having received a furlough from the military to go and plead his case, he went to the White House, approached the front gate and asked to see the president.

The guard on duty told him, "You can't see the president, young man! Don't you know there's a war going on? The president is a very busy man! Now go away, son! Get back out there on the battle lines where you belong!"

So the young soldier left, very disheartened, and was sitting on a little park bench not far from the White House when a little boy came up to him. The lad said, "Soldier, you look unhappy. What's wrong?" The soldier looked at the little boy and began to spill his heart to him. He told of his father and his brother being killed in the war, and of the desperate situation at home. He explained that his mother and sister had no one to help them with the farm. The little boy listened and said, "I can help you, soldier." He took the soldier by the hand and led him back to the front gate of the White House. Apparently, the guard didn't notice them, because they weren't stopped. They walked straight to the front door of the White House and walked right in. After they got inside, they walked right past generals and high-ranking officials, and no one said a word. The soldier couldn't understand this. Why didn't anyone try to stop them?

Finally, they reached the Oval Office—where the president was working—and the little boy didn't even knock on the door. He just walked right in and led the soldier in with him. There behind the desk was Abraham Lincoln and his Secretary of State, looking over battle plans that were laid out on his desk.

The president looked at the boy and then at the soldier and said, "Good afternoon, Todd. Can you introduce me to your friend?"

And Todd Lincoln, the son of the president, said, "Daddy, this soldier needs to talk to you."

The soldier pled his case before Mr. Lincoln, and right then and there he received the exemption that he desired.

✓ APPLICATION

We have access to the Father because of Jesus Christ, who intercedes for us. Because of Christ, we have peace with God. We can come to him anytime, anywhere. "But now in Christ Jesus you who once were far away have been brought near through the blood of Christ. For he himself is our peace, who has made the two one and has destroyed the barrier, the dividing wall of hostility . . . For through him we have access to the Father" (Ephesians 2:13, 18).

The Puppy Nobody Wanted

The sign on the door said "PUPPIES FOR SALE" and so the little boy went inside to look. The man inside the pet shop showed him five little puppies who were ready now to leave their mother. They were about the cutest dogs the little boy had ever seen.

"How much are they?" the little boy asked.

The man replied, "Some are fifty dollars, some are more."

The little boy reached into his pocket and pulled out some change. After counting it, he said, "I have a dollar and forty-seven cents."

"Well, I'm afraid I can't sell you one of these puppies for a dollar and forty-seven cents, little boy. You'll have to save your money and come back next time we have more puppies for sale."

About that time, the pet store owner's wife brought out another puppy that had been hidden in the back of the store. It was smaller than the other puppies, and had a bad leg. It couldn't stand up very well, and when it tried to walk, it limped very badly.

"What's wrong with that puppy?" asked the little boy. The pet store owner explained that the veterinarian had examined the puppy and had discovered it didn't have a hip socket. It would always limp and always be lame.

"Oh I wish I had the money to buy that puppy!" exclaimed the little boy with excitement. "That's the puppy I would choose!"

"Well that puppy is not for sale, son. But if you really want him, I'll just give him to you. No charge."

But the little boy got quite upset at this. He looked straight at the pet store owner and said, "No, I don't want you to give him to me. That little dog is worth every bit as much as the other dogs you have for sale. I'll give you a dollar and forty-seven cents now, and I'll give you fifty cents a month until I have paid for this dog in full."

The pet store owner was perplexed. "You don't really want to spend your money on this little dog, son. He is never going to be able to run and play with you like the other puppies."

Then the little boy reached down and rolled up his pant leg to reveal a badly twisted, crippled left leg, supported by a big metal brace. He looked up at the pet store owner and said, "Mister, I don't run and play too good myself. I figure this little puppy is going to need someone like me who understands."

✓ APPLICATION

Scripture says that you were "bought with a price." Jesus paid a very high price for you when he went to the cross. He did it because he loves you and wants you to be with him. And he understands what you are going through. As it says in the book of Isaiah, he was the "Suffering Servant" who "bore our iniquities." He took all of the pain we deserve upon himself.

You may feel like an outcast, a nobody. You may think nobody likes you, that nobody wants you. You may be suffering, going through difficult times. Through all of that, you can be sure that Jesus understands. He knows exactly how you feel.

THE QUAKER AND THE ATHEIST

Once upon a time, an atheist was arguing with a Quaker about the existence of God.

"Did you ever see God?" asked the atheist.

"No," said the Quaker.

"Did you ever smell God?" asked the atheist again.

"No," said the Quaker.

"Well, then," said the atheist with a smirk on his face." How can you be so sure that there is a God?"

"Friend, did thee ever see thy brains?" the Quaker asked the atheist.

"No," said the atheist.

"And did thee ever smell thy brains?" the Quaker asked again.

"No," answered the atheist.

"Dost thou believe that thou hast any brains?" asked the Quaker once more.

☑ APPLICATION

If you have any brains at all, you have to come to the inescapable conclusion that there is indeed a God—the brains behind this amazing world we call the universe. "No one has ever seen God," John reminds us in his gospel (1:18) but he has revealed himself to us in his creation, in his Word, and in the person and work of Jesus Christ.

RATS IN THE TUB

Several years ago, an experiment on endurance was conducted at the University of California at Berkeley involving Norwegian field rats. The rats were placed in a tub of water, where they were forced to swim until they grew exhausted and finally drowned. During the first experiment, the researchers discovered that on the average, Norwegian field rats were capable of swimming for over seven hours before drowning.

A second experiment was conducted, exactly like the first but with one exception. When a rat was getting too exhausted to swim any longer, the researchers would remove the rat from the tub of water for a few seconds, then put the rat back into the water to continue swimming. These rats were able to swim for almost twenty hours before perishing.

The researchers concluded that the rats in the second group were able to swim much longer than the first group because they had *hope*. They had experienced a rescue—and what kept them going was the *hope* that they would be rescued again.

☑ APPLICATION

Human beings are no different. Without hope, we drown. But with hope, we have a reason to live. Hope is what keeps us going. It has been said that "as oxygen is to the lungs, so hope is to the human heart."

Many people today have false hopes. They put their hopes in technology, or in hedonism, or in accumulating material wealth or power. But these hopes are like fool's gold; ultimately they are worthless and have no power to keep us afloat.

That's why Jesus came. He conquered death and the grave so that we would know that we also can do the same. This means *no matter what happens*, ultimately nothing can hurt us because we have victory in Christ Jesus. Christian hope is a *living* hope, "an inheritance that can never perish, spoil or fade, kept in heaven for you!" (1 Peter 1:3-4).

The Reasonable Hunter

Winter was coming on and a hunter went out into the forest to shoot a bear, out of which he planned to make a warm coat. By and by he saw a big bear coming toward him and raised his gun and took aim. "Wait," said the bear, "Why do you want to shoot me?"

"Because I am cold," said the hunter, "and I need a coat."

"But I am hungry," the bear replied, "so maybe if we just talk this over a little, we could come to a compromise."

So the hunter sat down beside the bear and began to talk over the pros and cons.

In the end, however, the hunter was well enveloped by the bear's fur, and the bear had eaten his dinner.

✓ APPLICATION

Sometimes we leave church or youth group or summer camp with great intentions. We are going to live for Jesus Christ, obey him in everything, resist temptation and in so doing, defeat Satan. We are "loaded up for bear!"

But we get out into the world and just as we are getting ready to take a stand for Jesus, Satan comes up and says, "Hey, let's talk this over. I think we can work this out so that you get what you want—and I get what I want. What do you say?"

Satan knows that we have a weapon—a double-edged sword called the Bible. We have the power to defeat Satan on the spot. But what often happens is we try to "deal with the devil," and ultimately it leads to our defeat.

When Jesus was tempted by Satan in the wilderness, he shot three bullets—all beginning with the phrase, "It is written . . . ". He quoted the Word of God and Satan had no power over him.

Don't bargain with the devil. If you do, you're dead meat.

146

THE ROADKILL GRILL

The Roadkill Grill Menu
"A Taste of the Wild"

Appetizers:
Fried Deer Hide
Riggermortis Tortoise
Awesome Possom Blossom
Critter Fritters
Bug Juice Soup

Rabbit of the Day
"Thumper on the Bumper"

Special: "Guess that Mess"
Guess what it is
and you eat free!

"Fender Lickin' Good"Entrees:
Chunk of Skunk
Rack of Racoon
Smear of Deer
Cheap Sheep
Flat Cat
Wreck of Lamb
Squeal Parmigiana
Robin on the Hood
Alley Cat-serole
Braked Chicken
Squiche Lorraine

Canine Cuisine
("You'll eat like a hog when you taste our dog!")
Poodles and Noodles
Slab of Lab
Cocker Cutlets
Ground Round Hound
Hushed Puppies

Desserts:
Road Toad Alamode
Armadillo Crunch

"Food is more fun when you hit it on the run!"

✔ APPLICATION

Unfortunately, many unsuspecting animals end up on the menu of the Roadkill Grill simply because they were in the wrong place at the wrong time. They were in the *middle of the road.*

And there are many young people who are in danger of becoming roadkill too. That's because they are "middle-of-the-road" Christians. They are neither on one side nor the other. They live for Christ when it's convenient, then live for themselves or for the crowd when that's more convenient. They are Christians on Sunday, but the rest of the week you can't really tell which side of the road they are on. They are middle-of-the-road Christians.

The Bible says, "Choose this day whom you will serve" (Joshua 24:15). Also: "No one can serve two masters. Either he will hate the one and love the other, or he will be devoted to the one and despise the other" (Matthew 6:24). And further: "So, because you are lukewarm—neither hot nor cold—I am about to spit you out of my mouth" (Revelation 3:16). All of these Scriptures make the point very clear. If you are a middle-of-the-road Christian, you are roadkill.

THE ROAR OF THE CROWD

On a balmy October afternoon in 1982, Badger Stadium in Madison, Wisconsin was packed. More than sixty thousand diehard University of Wisconsin fans were watching their football team take on Michigan State University. It soon became obvious that MSU had the better team. What seemed odd, however, as the score became more lopsided, were the burst of applause and shouts of joy from the Wisconsin fans. Even though their team was being pummeled on the field by the opposing team, they were smiling and high-fiving each other as if they were winning rather than losing. How could this be?

It turned out that seventy miles away, the Milwaukee Brewers were beating the St. Louis Cardinals in Game Three of the 1982 World Series. Many of the fans in the stands were listening to portable radios—and responding to something other than what they saw on the field.

✓ APPLICATION

How is it that Paul could write, " . . . For I delight in weaknesses, in insults, in hardships, in persecutions, in difficulties . . . ?" (1 Corinthians 12:10). He always seemed to have a positive attitude when things were going badly. Did he enjoy pain? Did he enjoy losing? No, not at all. But he was tuned in to another reality—he knew that even though he was experiencing bad news, he was in touch with the good news about Jesus Christ.

If your only reality is the world—what you see and hear all around you—you will become discouraged and begin to feel like a loser. But if you listen to the voice of God, you will be aware of a different reality—one that is cause for rejoicing. God is in control. In the midst of problems and difficulties, we know that "all things work together for good" to those who are tuned in to God (Romans 8:28).

SARGE

Years ago, a woman named Mary was severely burned while attempting to extinguish a grease fire on her stove. The scalding grease from her blazing frying pan left her with second and third-degree burns all over her arms and face.

Paramedics admitted Mary into the burn unit of the local hospital and a team of doctors began to administer treatment. Perhaps no pain is as excruciating as that of being burned, and no process more traumatic that of having to have skin grafted back onto your body. But Mary had to undergo a series of skin grafts that kept her in the hospital for several weeks.

In the midst of Mary's trauma, she met another patient who introduced himself simply as Sarge. It was obvious by looking at him that his burns had been far worse than hers, and she later heard stories of the incredibly painful skin grafts that had been done over most of his body. And yet this man was continually at her bedside, offering her a cup of coffee or some juice, asking if he could be of service. She discovered that he did this with many patients in the burn unit. Although his pain was probably the worst, he had somehow found within himself the ability to transcend it and serve others.

His positive attitude was contagious. He brought hope and life and love to a place filled with tragedy. Mary was amazed at his buoyant spirit and depth of compassion. She had been raised in the south, so she knew the importance of good manners and proper etiquette. But Sarge conveyed more than good manners. He was genuinely loving and kind.

He was a good man.

One evening Sarge came to Mary's bedside and they chatted for a while. He said with excitement that after a few more operations, he would be able to return home. He described how wonderful his children were and how proud he was of his wife, who had just graduated from college. Mary asked the name of the college, and when Sarge told her, she was stunned.

"Sarge, that's a *black* college," she said. "Your wife isn't black, is she?"

Sarge was quiet for a moment and then said, "Yes, ma'am. What color do you think I am?"

✓ APPLICATION

Like most of us, Mary probably didn't think of herself as a racist. But she discovered in a moment of embarrassment that she had made wrong assumptions about Sarge. How often do we do the same thing with people we meet?

Do you sometimes make wrong assumptions about people based on the color of their skin? Fortunately for all of us, God is color-blind. He created all of us—"red and yellow, black and white"—and he loves us all the same. What matters to God is not the color of your skin, but the condition of your soul. "The Lord does not look at the things man looks at. Man looks at the outward appearance, but the Lord looks at the heart" (1 Samuel 16:7).

Save the Starfish

There was once a little boy who was walking along the beach and all of a sudden he came upon thousands of starfish that had washed up on the beach. The tide was going out, and for some strange reason, the starfish ended up stuck on the beach. They were all doomed because they couldn't survive being out of the water in the hot sun until the next high tide. The little boy realized this and frantically started picking up starfish and throwing them, one at a time, back into the water.

A man who was walking along the beach saw the boy doing this and he yelled at the boy, "Son, what in the world are you doing? Don't you know that there are thousands of starfish on this beach? And don't you know that this beach goes on for miles and miles? There is no way in the world you can save all those starfish!"

The little boy thought about that for a moment, then turned to the man, picked up a starfish and said, "Yeah, I know. But I can save *this* one."

And he heaved it as far as he could into the ocean.

✓ APPLICATION

Sometimes we get discouraged because we can't solve all the problems of the world, or see all of our friends and family come to Christ, or do everything that we feel God wants us to do.

But we can do *something*. And something is always better than doing nothing at all.

You aren't going to be able to win the whole world to Christ. But you can share the love of Jesus with one person. Scripture tells us that all of heaven rejoices when just one person is saved.

You can't do everything—but you can do a lot more than you think you can. And God will take what you do, bless it, and multiply it—just like he did with a little boy's lunch beside the sea of Galilee.

So pick up a starfish and throw it. That's all God wants you to do. He'll do the rest.

THE SEAGULL

Imagine this scene: You are on the Florida coast. The sun is setting like a gigantic orange ball. It's the cool evening on a vacant, isolated stretch of beach. The water is lapping at the shore, the breeze is blowing slightly. There are one or two joggers and a couple of fishermen. Most people have gone home for the day.

You look up and you see an old man with curved shoulders, bushy eyebrows, and bony features hobbling down the beach carrying a bucket. He carries the bucket up to the pier, a dock that goes out into the water. He stands on the dock and you notice he is looking up into the sky and all of a sudden you see a mass of dancing dots. You soon recognize that they are seagulls. They are coming out of nowhere. The man takes out of his bucket handfuls of shrimp and begins to throw them on the dock. The seagulls come and land all around him. Some land on his shoulders, some land on his hat, and they eat the shrimp. Long after the shrimp are gone his feathered friends linger. The old man and the birds.

What is going on here? Why is this man feeding seagulls? What could compel him to do this—as he does week after week?

The man in that scene was Eddie Rickenbacher, a famous World War II pilot. His plane, *The Flying Fortress*, went down in 1942 and no one thought he would be rescued. Perhaps you have read or heard how he and his eight passengers escaped death by climbing into two rafts for thirty days. They fought thirst, the sun, and sharks. Some of the sharks were nine feet long. The boats were only eight feet long. But what nearly killed them was starvation. Their rations were gone within eight days and they didn't have anything left.

Rickenbacher wrote that even on those rafts, every day they would have a daily afternoon devotional and prayer time. One day after the devotional, Rickenbacher leaned back and put his hat over his eyes and tried to get some sleep. Within a few moments he felt something on his head. He knew in an instant it was a seagull which had perched on his raft. But he knew that they were hundreds of miles out to sea. Where did this seagull come from? He was also certain that if he didn't get that seagull he would die. Soon all the others on the two boats noticed the seagull. No one spoke, no one moved. Rickenbacher quickly grabbed the seagull and with thanksgiving, they ate the flesh of the bird. They used the intestines for fish bait and survived.

Rickenbacher never forgot that visitor who came from a foreign place. That sacrificial guest. Every week, he went out on the pier with a bucket of shrimp and said thank you, thank you, thank you.

✓ APPLICATION

The apostle Paul wrote, "For Christ's love compels us . . . " (2 Corinthians 5:14). The word "compels" means literally, "leaves me no choice." Paul is saying, "I have no choice but to respond to the love of Christ with my whole being—to say thank you, thank you, thank you!"

When we serve Christ, when we share God's love with others, when we come to church each week to worship him, we don't do it begrudgingly. We do it with thankful hearts because we really have no choice. It's how we say thank you!

SHARPEN YOUR AX

A young man approached the foreman of a logging crew and asked for a job. "That depends," replied the foreman. "Let's see you fell this tree." The young man stepped forward, and skillfully felled a great tree. Impressed, the foreman exclaimed, "You can start Monday."

Monday, Tuesday, Wednesday, Thursday rolled by—and Thursday afternoon the foreman approached the young man and said, "You can pick up your paycheck on the way out today."

Startled, the young man replied, "I thought you paid on Friday."

"Normally we do," said the foreman. "But we're letting you go today because you've fallen behind. Our daily felling charts show that you've dropped from first place on Monday to last place today."

"But I'm a hard worker," the young man objected. "I arrive first, leave last, and even have worked through my coffee breaks!"

"The foreman, sensing the young man's integrity, thought for a minute and then asked, "Have you been sharpening your ax?"

"The young man replied, "No sir. I've been working too hard to take time for that!"

✓ APPLICATION

Our lives are like that. We sometimes get so busy that we don't take time to "sharpen the ax." In today's world, it seems that everyone is busier than ever, but less happy than ever. Why is that? Could it be that we have forgotten how to stay sharp?

There's nothing wrong with activity and hard work. But God doesn't want us to get so busy that we neglect the truly important things in life, like taking time to pray, to read and study Scripture, or to listen to "the still small voice of God." We all need time to relax, to think and meditate, to learn and grow. If we don't take time to sharpen the ax, we will become dull and lose our effectiveness.

SQUIRT SQUIRT

The Danish philosopher Soren Kierkegaard once wrote about a town where a fireman lived. Everyone liked the fireman because he was a nice guy. He made it a habit to be gentle and kind, which was unusual for firemen, who were supposed to be tough.

There was a fire one day, and the fireman charged to the scene of the fire with his fellow firemen and heavy equipment. As they came toward the fire, much to their surprise and chagrin, they encountered between themselves and the flames about two hundred townspeople. And each of them was standing there with a water pistol, aiming at the fire, going squirt, squirt, squirt, squirt.

The fireman asked, "What's going on here?" A spokesman for the group turned and said, "Well, we all appreciate this wonderful work you're doing in our community, and each of us has come to contribute in some small way to your work." Squirt, squirt.

The fireman said, "I don't get it. You are all crazy!"

"Oh we realize that we all could do more, couldn't we, folks?" said the spokesman.

"Most definitely," everyone said, "But we just wanted to offer this token of our support." Squirt, squirt.

"You don't know what you're doing!" shouted the fireman.

"True, but you have to appreciate the fact that everyone is willing to offer whatever help they can," said the spokesman.

And everyone said, "Amen!" and went squirt, squirt.

At that, the fireman shouted, "Get the #*#! out of her e! This is no picnic, this is a fire, and a fire doesn't require well-meaning people who come to make small contributions. A fire is a place where people come to give their lives."

✓ APPLICATION

Sometimes we are a lot like those people:

"We all appreciate the work you're doing, pastor." Squirt, squirt. "We want to let you know that we support all that you're trying to do." Squirt, squirt. "We bring what we can—it's not much, but the little bit we can offer to the work of the kingdom we gladly give." Squirt, squirt.

And one hears the celestial fireman say, "Will you please get out of here! What I am looking for are disciples who are radically committed and willing to die for the sake of the gospel!"

Following Jesus means being willing to follow him to the cross. "And anyone who does not take his cross and follow me is not worthy of me. Whoever finds his life will lose it, and whoever loses his life for my sake will find it" (Matthew 10:38-39).

SMART HOPIS

Not long after the I.Q. (Intelligence Quotient) test was developed, several studies were conducted to find out how different groups of people scored on the test as groups. The test was administered to men and women, young and old, rich and poor, and many ethnic groups as well. It was in this context that the I.Q. test was given to a group of Hopi Indians.

When the Hopi received the test, they immediately started to ask each other questions and to compare their answers. The instructor saw this happening, and quickly intervened, telling them that they each had to take the test alone. "You are not permitted to help each other or to share your answers among yourselves," he told them.

When the Hopi heard this, they were outraged and refused to take the test, saying, "It is not important that I am smarter than my brother, or that my brother is smarter than me. It is only important what we can do together!"

☑ APPLICATION

Unfortunately, we live in a world that puts a big emphasis on what we do alone. As a result, we suffer from all sorts of maladies: low self-esteem, competitiveness, jealousy, greed, anger, and hostility, to name a few.

But God created us to live in community with each other—to work together, to share our resources with each other, to help each other out. The principle is love, not competitiveness and greed. In the body of Christ, no one is greater or more important than anyone else (see 1 Corinthians 12). Christianity is not a religion for "Lone Rangers." We really do need each other.

STEPHEN'S EGG

It was obvious that eight-year-old Stephen's mental retardation was becoming even more severe. His Sunday school teacher did her best to include Stephen in the classroom activities and to avoid situations which might prompt his classmates to make fun of him.

In April, she gave each of the eight children in the class an empty L'eggs pantyhose container (plastic egg) and instructed them to place inside the container an object that represented new life in spring. Fearing that Stephen might not have caught on, and not wanting to embarrass him, the teacher had the children place all the containers on the desk so that she could open them.

The first had a tiny flower in it. "What a lovely sign of new life," said the teacher. One of the students couldn't help but erupt, "I brought that one!"

Next came a rock. The teacher assumed this must be Stephen's, since rocks don't symbolize new life. But Billy shouted that his rock had moss on it, and moss represented new life. "Very good, Billy," agreed the teacher.

A butterfly flew from the third container and another child bragged that her choice was the best of all.

The fourth container was empty. This must be Stephen's, thought the teacher, quickly reaching for a different one.

"Teacher, please don't skip mine," interrupted Stephen.

"But it's empty, Stephen." said the teacher gently.

"That's right," said Stephen. "The tomb was empty, and that represents new life for everyone."

Later that summer, Stephen's condition worsened and he died. At his funeral on his casket, mourners found eight L'eggs pantyhose containers, all of them empty.

☑ APPLICATION

The true story of Stephen reminds us of the hope we all have because of the resurrection of Jesus Christ. "For as in Adam all die, so in Christ all will be made alive" (1 Corinthians 15:22).

TEAR IT DOWN

A businessman owned a warehouse which had sat empty for months and needed repairs. Vandals had damaged the doors, smashed the windows, and trash was everywhere inside the building.

The businessman showed a prospective buyer the property and took great pains to say that he would replace the broken windows, bring in a crew to correct any structural damage and clean out all the garbage.

"Forget about the repairs," the buyer said. "When I buy this place, I'm going to build something completely different, something entirely new. I don't want the building. I just want the site!"

☑ APPLICATION

Compared with the renovation that God has in mind, our efforts to improve our own lives are as trivial as sweeping out a warehouse slated for the wrecking ball. When you become a Christian, the "old is passed away; the new has come!" (2 Corinthians 5:17).

You can't keep your "old building" when you come to Jesus. He doesn't want the building—but he does want the site. The site is the real you—the you that was created in the image of God. And the old building—with its dark rooms and bad habits—is demolished. You become a new creation in Christ Jesus.

TOO HELPFUL

During the French Revolution, there were three Christians who were sentenced to die by the guillotine. One Christian had the gift of faith, the other had the gift of prophecy, the other had the gift of being helpful (or the gift of helps).

The Christian with the gift of faith was to be executed first. He was asked if he wanted to wear a hood over his head. He declined and said he was not afraid to die. "I have faith that God will deliver me!" he shouted bravely. His head was positioned under the guillotine, with his neck on the chopping block. He looked up at the sharp blade, said a short prayer and waited confidently. The rope was pulled, but nothing happened. His executioners were amazed and, believing that this must have been an act of God, they freed the man.

The Christian with the gift of prophecy was next. His head was positioned under the guillotine blade and he too was asked if he wanted the hood. "No," he said, "I am not afraid to die. However, I predict that God will deliver me from this guillotine!" At that, the rope was pulled and again, nothing happened. Once again, the puzzled executioners assumed this must be a miracle of God, and they freed the man.

The third Christian, with the gift of being helpful, was next. He was brought to the guillotine and likewise asked if he wanted to wear a hood. "No," he said, "I'm just as brave as those other two guys." The executioners then positioned him face up under the guillotine and were about to pull the rope when the man stopped them. "Hey wait a minute," he said. "I think I just found the problem with your guillotine."

☑ APPLICATION

We all have spiritual gifts, but we need to know when to use them.

TOO MUCH PRAYER?

Johnny, a very bright five-year-old, told his daddy he'd like to have a baby brother and, along with his request, offered to do whatever he could to help. His dad, a very bright thirty-five-year-old, paused for a moment and then replied, "I'll tell you what, Johnny. If you pray every day for two months for a baby brother, I guarantee that God will give you one!" Johnny responded eagerly to his dad's challenge and went to his bedroom early that night to start praying for a baby brother.

He prayed every night for a whole month, but after that time, he began to get skeptical. He checked around the neighborhood and found out that what he thought was going to happen had never occurred in the history of the neighborhood. You just don't pray for two months and then, whammo—a new baby brother. So, Johnny quit praying. After another month, Johnny's mother went to the hospital. When she came back home, Johnny's parents called him into the bedroom. He cautiously walked into the room, not expecting to find anything, and there was a little bundle lying right next to his mother. His dad pulled back the blanket and there was—not one baby brother—but two! His mother had twins! Johnny's dad looked down at him and said, "Now aren't you glad you prayed?" Johnny hesitated a little and then looked up at his dad and said, "Yes, but aren't you glad I quit when I did?"

✓ APPLICATION

Johnny's dad knew in advance that Johnny's prayer would be answered. And our heavenly Father knows in advance whether or not our prayers will be answered too. He can see the future. And the Bible also tells us that God knows our wants and needs, even before we ask. So why pray?

First of all, God wants us to demonstrate faith in him. He wants us to demonstrate our dependence upon him. So Jesus taught us to pray, "Give us this day our daily bread." God knows that we need food and clothing and good health and even baby brothers (sometimes). But he wants us to come to him in prayer anyhow. Prayer is a powerful thing. Our prayers do matter! They are not just exercises in faith. Yes, God knows what the future holds, but if we don't pray, we forfeit our right to influence the future and to agree with God on what our future will be. He eagerly awaits hearing from you.

True or False?

On the Internet, there is a news group in which readers post "urban myths" and discuss whether or not they are true, false or unanswerable. Below are some of the myths that have been discussed on the Internet and conclusions that have been drawn about them. What do you think? Are they true or false?

1. A penny dropped from the top of the Empire State Building will embed itself in the pavement. (*false*)
2. The bubbles in bubble-wrap (the packing material) contain a toxic gas. (*false*)
3. You can send a coconut through the mail without wrapping it. (*true*)
4. If the entire population of China jumped up and down at the same time, the earth's orbit would be disturbed. (*false*)
5. Welding while wearing contact lenses will cause the lenses to stick to your eyeballs. (*false*)
6. Unless marked "dairy," fast-food shakes aren't milk, but mostly carrageen gel. (*true*)
7. If your college roommate commits suicide, you get automatic *A*s in all your courses. (*false*)
8. A woman was impregnated by swimming in a pool with loose sperm. (*false*)

9. Koalas are always stoned (drunk) from ingesting the alcohol in eucalyptus leaves. (*false*)

10. Albert Einstein did poorly in school. (*false*)

11. A woman adopted a stray dog in Tijuana, Mexico and later discovered it was a sewer rat. (*false*)

12. Some Oregon highway workers blew up a whale and showered the town with whale blubber. (*true*)

13. Some people like to eat the placenta of their children. (*true*)

14. A mime had a heart attack during his act. The audience thought it was part of the act and did nothing. He died. (*false*)

15. *Bubble Yum* bubble gum is made with spider eggs. (*false*)

16. You can tell if a big operation is under way at the White House by the level of pizza orders that come from there. (*false*)

✓ APPLICATION

In today's world, it's hard sometimes to determine the true from the false. Some things sound true, but they are only myths. Other things seem hard to believe, but they are absolutely true. And many times, there's no way to know which is which.

Myths come and go. But truth endures forever. That's one reason the Word of God has survived for thousands of years. No other document has stood the test of time like the Holy Bible. Generation after generation has found that God's Word is true. It can be trusted.

Two Scoops of Anti-freeze, Lice-Killer with Chocolate Sauce!

Have you ever thought about what you're putting in your mouth when you eat that delicious ice cream sundae? Never mind the calories or the fat grams—we're talking about some serious ingredients.

For example, today's commercial ice cream usually substitutes dimethyl glycol instead of eggs—a chemical that is also used in anti-freeze and paint remover. Most of the time, piperonal is substituted for vanilla, but it's also used in larger quantities to kill lice. And then, when you top off that sundae with strawberry flavor, remember that you are probably ingesting benzyl acetate, a chemical that is used as a solvent for nitrate, one of the main ingredients in fertilizers and cheap explosives.

This information shouldn't stop us from eating ice cream or make us want to start boycotting Dairy Queen. Ice cream is fine and wonderful as long as we enjoy it the way it was designed by its creator. But if we just decide that we are hungry for ice cream and start scarfing down anti-freeze and lice medicine, we would probably die (although it might be with a nice clean scalp, and a circulation system that is not affected by cold weather!).

Why would we die? Because we are attempting to quench a normal desire for ice cream in a way that was never intended by the designer.

Lust can be an awful lot like ice cream.

You see, lust is any desire which leads us to satisfy a normal hunger in a way never intended by our designer. Lust is what happens when good God-given appetites consume us, control us and become our point of focus—so that we try to satisfy that God-given appetite in a way God did not design. Maybe sex outside of marriage has some of the same ingredients, and it may not seem that harmful right away, but that's never way the designer intended it.

God never said "Sex is bad" any more than he ever said "Thou shalt not eateth ice creameth." But God makes it clear that this God-given desire for sexual intimacy must be fulfilled within God-given guidelines. Or, the result can be poisoned lives and poisoned relationships.

UNBAPTIZED ARMS

Ivan the Terrible was one of the great Czars of sixteenth-century Russia—best known for his erratic behavior and his brutality. He was so busy conquering new territory for his country that he had no time to find a wife. His advisors became concerned that he had not married, and therefore would not produce an heir to the throne. So Ivan commanded his men to find him a suitable wife who was beautiful, intelligent, and the daughter of a nobleman.

They found her in Greece. Her name was Sophia, the daughter of the king of Greece. Ivan asked the king for his daughter's hand in marriage and the king agreed on the condition that Ivan be baptized and join the church. Ivan agreed and set out for Greece to be married, accompanied by five hundred of his best soldiers.

When they discovered that Ivan was to be baptized, the solders said they wanted to be baptized also. A requirement of baptism was to make a profession of faith and to affirm the articles of the Orthodox church, which the soldiers agreed to do—except for one. The article they couldn't affirm was one which prohibited them from being professional soldiers. They asked the priest if they could have some time to think over the problem of how to join the church and at the same time remain soldiers in Ivan's army.

They devised a plan among themselves and announced that they were ready to be baptized. They marched out into the water, all five hundred of them, with five hundred priests. As the priests put the soldiers under the water, each soldier grasped his sword and lifted it high in the air. The soldiers were baptized completely, except for their swords and their fighting arms. Those who witnessed the mass baptism said that it was an amazing spectacle to see five hundred dry arms and five hundred swords sticking up out of the water.

✓ APPLICATION

The soldiers had decided that they could give all of themselves to the church except for their fighting arms and their swords. These would remain in possession of the state.

Some of us today are no different from those soldiers. We want to become Christians and to possess the promise of eternal life. We want the blessing of God on our lives and to be part of his forever family, the church. But we want it on our terms. So we come to Christ with one arm up out of the water. In our hands, we hold those things we are unwilling to let go of— our possessions, our time, our money, our friends, our bad habits. But Paul writes in Romans 12, "I urge you . . . in view of God's mercy, to offer your bodies as living sacrifices, holy and pleasing to God." We must offer to God our whole selves—not just part of us.

What part of your life have you been unwilling to give to God? What is the "unbaptized arm" in your life?

WHAT WILL MY REWARD BE?

One day a fisherman was lying on a beautiful beach, with his fishing pole propped up in the sand and his solitary line cast out into the sparkling blue surf. He was enjoying the warmth of the afternoon sun and the prospect of catching a fish.

About that time, a businessman came walking down the beach, trying to relieve some of the stress of his workday. He noticed the fisherman sitting on the beach and decided to find out why this fisherman was fishing instead of working harder to make a living for himself and his family. "You aren't going to catch many fish that way," said the businessman to the fisherman. "You should be working rather than lying on the beach!"

The fisherman looked up at the businessman, smiled and replied, "And what will my reward be?"

"Well, you can get bigger nets and catch more fish!" was the businessman's answer.

"And then what will my reward be?" asked the fisherman, still smiling.

The businessman replied, "You will make money and you'll be able to buy a boat, which will then result in larger catches of fish!"

"And then what will my reward be?" asked the fisherman again.

The businessman was beginning to get a little irritated with the fisherman's questions. "You can buy a bigger boat, and hire some people to work for you!" he said.

"And then what will my reward be?" repeated the fisherman.

The businessman was getting angry. "Don't you understand? You can build up a fleet of fishing boats, sail all over the world, and let all your employees catch fish for you!"

Once again the fisherman asked, "And then what will my reward be?"

The businessman was red with rage and shouted at the fisherman, "Don't you understand that you can become so rich that you will never have to work for your living again! You can spend all the rest of your days sitting on this beach, looking at the sunset. You won't have a care in the world!"

The fisherman, still smiling, looked up and said, "And what do you think I'm doing right now?"

☑ APPLICATION

There are many people who work extremely hard during their lives to achieve happiness. They work hard to accumulate enough money to buy the happiness that they want.

But as the story illustrates, there is something inherently wrong with that approach to life.

What is the real reward that comes from working? The businessman in the story never satisfactorily answered that question.

According to Scripture, we work to bring glory to God. Work is one of the ways we worship God. Paul wrote in Colossians, "Whatever you do, work at it with all your heart, as working for the Lord, not for men." True happiness comes from serving God, not from accumulating wealth. "Whatever you do," writes Paul, "do it all in the name of the Lord Jesus, giving thanks to God the Father through him" (Colossians 3:17). Our reward is that God is glorified and we are fulfilled as human beings—because that's what we were created to do.

WHEN NOTHING GOES RIGHT

A young man was learning to be a paratrooper. Before his first jump, he was given these instructions:

1. Jump when you are told.

2. Count to ten and pull the ripcord.

3. In the unlikely event your parachute doesn't open, pull the emergency ripcord.

4. When you get down, a truck will be there to take you back to the airport.

The young man memorized these instructions and climbed aboard the plane. The plane climbed to ten thousand feet and the paratroopers began to jump. When the young man was told to jump, he jumped. He then counted to ten and pulled the ripcord. Nothing happened. His chute failed to open. So he pulled the emergency ripcord. Still, nothing happened. No parachute.

"Oh great," said the young man. "And I suppose the truck won't be there when I get down either!"

☑ APPLICATION

Have you ever felt like that young man? Have you had so many failures and disappointments in life that you just don't expect anything to go right for you?

Well, unlike the young man in our story, there is hope. In Jesus Christ, we can be forgiven for the failures of the past and we can start all over. Christianity is sometimes called the "gospel of the second chance" because our failures never have to be fatal. That's what the grace of God is all about. Even though our parachutes fail to open, we can always fall into the loving arms of our heavenly Father.

WHO, ME?

There was once a college student who was struggling in many areas of his life. He spent a great deal of his time feeling angry and frustrated. When he could stand it no longer, he went to the dim and seldom-used chapel on campus. He paced up and down the aisles, slapping the back of the empty

pews. He yelled, he cried, and he raged at God.

"God you created the world . . . what could you possibly have been thinking? Look at the problems people face. Look at the pain, suffering, and hunger. Look at the neglect, the waste, the abuse. Everywhere I look, I see messed-up people, hurting people, lonely people!" The young man ranted and raved on and on.

Finally, exhausted, he sat in the front pew and looked hopelessly at the cross. Its tarnished surface reflected the dusty sunlight filtering in through the stained glass windows. "It's all such a mess! This world you created is nothing but a terrible mess! Why even I could make a world better than this one!"

And then the young man heard a voice in the silence of that dusty chapel that made his eyes open wide and his jaw drop.

"And that is exactly what I want you to do."

✓ APPLICATION

It's easy to identify problems that exist all around us. And sometimes we wonder why God doesn't solve them all for us. But that's why God created the church. That's why God put you here—at this particular time and place. He has gifted you and given you the power to make a difference in the world.

God has commissioned the church to be the hands and feet of Jesus in a broken world. That's why we are called "the body of Christ." Will you do your part?

Wolves o' Plenty

An organization in Montana offered a bounty of five thousand dollars for every wolf captured alive. Two hunters named Sam and Jed decided to head for the hills and make some money capturing wolves. Day and night they scoured the mountains and forests searching for their valuable prey. Exhausted after three days of hunting without any success, they both fell asleep.

During the night, Sam suddenly woke up to find that he and Jed were surrounded by a pack of fifty wolves, with flaming red eyes and bared teeth, snarling at the two hunters and preparing to pounce.

Sam nudged Jed and said, "Hey, wake up! We're gonna be rich!"

✓ APPLICATION

Sometimes when we are surrounded by what appears to be many difficulties, we may in fact be surrounded by many opportunities. The Chinese symbol for the word "crisis" actually combines the two words "danger" and "opportunity." When a crisis occurs, we can choose to be frightened and cowardly, or strong and courageous. It's all a matter of perspective.

Next time you find yourself in a jam, remember: "You're gonna be rich!" You have the opportunity to learn and grow, and to experience the grace and power of God in that situation. Situations like that don't come along every day!

You Know the Psalm

There was once a Shakespearian actor who was known far and wide for his one-man show of readings and recitations from the classics. He would always end his performance with a dramatic reading of the Twenty-third Psalm. Each night, without exception, as the actor began his recitation—*The Lord is my shepherd, I shall not want*—the crowd would listen attentively. And then, at the conclusion of the psalm, they would rise in thunderous applause in appreciation of the actor's incredible ability to bring the verse to life.

But one night, just before the actor was to offer his customary recital of Psalm Twenty-three, a young man from the audience spoke up. "Sir, do you mind if tonight I recite the Twenty-third Psalm?"

The actor was quite taken back by this unusual request, but he allowed the young man to come forward and stand front and center on the stage to recite the psalm, knowing that the ability of this unskilled youth would be no match for his own talent.

With a soft voice, the young man began to recite the words of the Psalm. When he was finished, there was no applause. There was no standing ovation as on other nights. All that could be heard was the sound of weeping. The audience had been so moved by the young man's recitation, that every eye was full of tears.

Amazed by what he heard, the actor said to the youth, "I don't understand. I have been performing the Twenty-third Psalm for years. I have a lifetime of experience and training—but I have never been able to move as audience as you have tonight. Tell me, what is your secret?"

The young man humbly replied, "Well sir, you know the psalm . . . *but I know the shepherd.*"

✓ APPLICATION

It's not enough to just know the content of the Bible—its stories, its sayings, and its teachings. Unless you know the author, the Bible is nothing more than just another book. But when put your faith in Jesus Christ and have entered into a personal relationship with God the Father, the Bible truly becomes "living and active—sharper than any double-edged sword" (Hebrews 4:12).

The Zurka Bird

Two wealthy brothers set out one Christmas to purchase the very best Christmas present they could find for their mother. The search for this present became so fierce that the two brothers turned it into a contest to see who could find the most unique and extraordinary present that was available. One brother thought he had found the perfect present. He found a Zurka bird.

Now the Zurka bird was no ordinary bird. It was a very rare and special bird. Costing many thousands of dollars, it had to be flown in from the Amazon. It could speak five different languages. It could recite beautiful poetry and sing opera. It was an amazing bird, indeed.

So the brother paid dearly for the Zurka bird, wrapped it carefully and had it sent to his mother for Christmas. On Christmas day, he gave his mother plenty of time to wake up, eat breakfast, and open his gift. Finally he could wait no longer. He called his mother and when she picked up the telephone, he almost shouted into the phone, "Mother, mother, what did you think about the beautiful Zurka bird that I sent you??"

On the other end of the line, the mother had this reply: "Oh, son, it was delicious!"

✓ APPLICATION

God has given to us some wonderfully unique gifts. Unfortunately, we sometimes don't realize how wonderful they are and we end up misusing them or doing great damage to them. Take the gift of sex for example. Sex is a wonderful gift that was meant to be enjoyed by two people who have committed themselves to each other and to God in marriage. Just as the woman ate the Zurka bird (which was delicious) and never really enjoyed it as intended, there are many people who eat up sex (which is also delicious) and never really enjoy it as God intended.

God has given us many other gifts as well—and he wants us to use them for their intended purpose (1 Corinthians 12, Ephesians 4, Romans 12). And then there is Jesus Christ, God's greatest gift of all (2 Corinthians 9:15). Do you appreciate God's gifts to you?

Index to Topics

Index of Contributors

Doug Adams
Jesus' Family Tree

Tony Campolo
The Animal School
Make Me Like Joe
The New Gorilla

Les Christie
A Candle in the Darkness
A Stranger at the Door
The Balloon Man
The Beggar
Blackout!
The Dead Cat
Fishing Eagles
G.I. Life Insurance
Get Off My Back
The Lantern
The Mud Flats
Nobel's Legacy
The Seagull
Squirt Squirt

Gary Clark
The King's Driver

Derek Combs
The Great Dane and the Alligator
Not-So-Identical Twins
The Zurka Bird

Jeff Crosby
The Painting in the Warehouse

Bob Faulhaber, Jr.
The Face on the Puzzle

Doug Fields
A Million Frogs
Are You God?
The Burning Hut
But Is He Safe?
Great Answers but No Help
The Logic Exam
Lost and Found
The Milkman's Gift
The Quaker and the Atheist
The Reasonable Hunter
The Roar of the Crowd
Too Much Prayer?

Dave Hampson
Grandma's Gift

Carson Henley
Alligators in Your Pond

Don Holliday
One More Year
The President and the Little Boy

Premek Kramerius
What Will My Reward Be?

Scott Longyear
You Know the Psalm

Joel Lusz
A Visit from Space
The Bridge Operator
When Nothing Goes Right

Brennan Manning
A Vision of Jesus
The Empty Chair

Sonny Martini
The Native American
  and the Rattlesnake

Bill McNabb
Chippie's Bad Day
I Ain't Lost
Inside the Fence
Life Inside the Womb
The Mice in the Piano
Rats in the Tub
Smart Hopis
Stephen's Egg
Tear It Down
Unbaptized Arms

Miles McPherson
Jimmy and the Genie

Scott Meier
Who, Me?

Marty Milligan
Grab a What?

Jeff Mugford
Wolves o' Plenty

Laurie Polich
The Evangelist and the Post Office
Love and the Cabbie

Mike Sciarra
The Emperor's Seeds

Duffy Robbins
The Devil's Triangle
"Excuse Me" or "Forgive Me"?
Fake Christians
The Horse Trader
Just a Hyphen
Two Scoops of Anti-Freeze,
    Lice-Killer with Chocolate Sauce

Doug Webster
The Keeper of the Spring